5000

Layman's Bible Book Commentary
1 & 2 Samuel, 1 Chronicles

LAYMAN'S BIBLE BOOK COMMENTARY

LBBC

1 & 2 SAMUEL, 1 CHRONICLES

VOLUME 5

Joe O. Lewis

BROADMAN PRESS
Nashville, Tennessee

© Copyright 1980 • Broadman Press.

All rights reserved.

4211-75

ISBN: 0-8054-1175-5

Dewey Decimal Classification: 222.4

Subject headings: BIBLE. O. T. SAMUEL//
BIBLE. O. T. 1 CHRONICLES

Library of Congress Catalog Card Number: 80-67148

Printed in the United States of America

Foreword

The *Layman's Bible Book Commentary* in twenty-four volumes was planned as a practical exposition of the whole Bible for lay readers and students. It is based on the conviction that the Bible speaks to every generation of believers but needs occasional reinterpretation in the light of changing language and modern experience. Following the guidance of God's Spirit, the believer finds in it the authoritative word for faith and life.

To meet the needs of lay readers, the *Commentary* is written in a popular style, and each Bible book is clearly outlined to reveal its major emphases. Although the writers are competent scholars and reverent interpreters, they have avoided critical problems and the use of original languages except where they were essential for explaining the text. They recognize the variety of literary forms in the Bible, but they have not followed documentary trails or become preoccupied with literary concerns. Their primary purpose was to show what each Bible book meant for its time and what it says to our own generation.

The Revised Standard Version of the Bible is the basic text of the *Commentary*, but writers were free to use other translations to clarify an occasional passage or sharpen its effect. To provide as much interpretation as possible in such concise books, the Bible text was not printed along with the comment.

Of the twenty-four volumes of the *Commentary*, fourteen deal with Old Testament books and ten with those in the New Testament. The volumes range in pages from 140 to 168. Four major books in the Old Testament and five in the New are treated in one volume each. Others appear in various combinations. Although the allotted space varies, each Bible book is treated as a whole to reveal its basic message with some passages getting special attention. Whatever plan of Bible study the reader may follow, this *Commentary* will be a valuable companion.

Despite the best-seller reputation of the Bible, the average survey of Bible knowledge reveals a good deal of ignorance about it and its primary meaning. Many adult church members seem to think that its study is intended for children and preachers. But some of the newer translations have been making the Bible more readable for all ages. Bible study has branched out from Sunday into other days of the week, and into neighborhoods rather than just in churches This *Commentary* wants to meet the growing need for insight into all that the Bible has to say about God and his world and about Christ and his fellowship.

BROADMAN PRESS

Contents

1 SAMUEL

2 SAMUEL

1 CHRONICLES

1 & 2 SAMUEL

Introduction

These two books bear the name of the great transition figure in Israel's history, a man who stood between two ages. Samuel bridged the gap between the tribal period and the age of the kings. His name was used as the title of the entire history because he was the first major character in the story and because he played such a powerful role in shaping Israel's destiny.

Authorship

No one knows who wrote the book of Samuel which we now use. Samuel, Nathan, and Gad may well have left accounts which were ultimately used in putting the whole together (1 Chron. 29:29). But the story looks back at these great figures and records their respective roles in the events that made Israel a kingdom. Their stories do not read as if they came from their own hands. We must be content to know that God chose and inspired a master theologian whom we can't identify to write this account of the development of David's kingship.

Date

The date of writing also remains shrouded in a maze of possibilities. The two books of Samuel originally formed one book in the Hebrew Bible. All Hebrew copies of these materials dating before the fifteenth century AD treat them as one book. The fact that the books of Samuel were written as a unit affects our decision about the date of writing. In fact, you will notice later that the story of Solomon's rise to power actually forms a part of the story told in Samuel, but it now comes in the book of Kings! So the date of Samuel even depends partly on the date of Kings. The story in Kings extends all the way into the period of the Babylonian captivity, to about 560 BC (2 Kings 25:27). Clearly the writer who finished the story lived after that time. However, there is every reason to believe that the books of Samuel were originally written centuries earlier and became part of the larger history later. A hard question is, When were the books of Samuel first composed? Since the story leads up to the crowning of Solomon in 1 Kings it seems likely that the original account came during or soon after Solomon's reign (960-922 BC). It is quite possible that the division of the two kingdoms about 922 BC provided part of the reason for the writing of Samuel. The Historian, as the writer will be called in this book, had access to memories dating at least one to two hundred years before his time, some of which doubtless were written.

Purpose

Many purposes may have helped shape the books of Samuel, but one overriding purpose dominates the whole. That purpose was to demonstrate the right of the Davidic kings to rule Judah and Israel, a right anchored in the will of God and established by the work of God. While it is easy for us to accept David's rule as the result of divine activity, it was not so easy for his contemporaries. Many refused to accept David's rule and that of his dynasty (2 Sam. 16:7; 20:1; 1 Kings 12:16). The Historian wrote to show that indeed God had taken David from following sheep and made him king. Moreover, he argued that God had made a special covenant with David's descendants that they should be the rulers of Judah and Israel.

Value

The Historian has shown the disastrous consequences of departing from the divine covenant. But he was not blind to the faults of God's chosen kings. He described them with brutal honesty (2 Sam. 11), thus demonstrating that it was not easy for the people to be faithful to a covenant which involved such "earthen vessels." Perhaps the greatest value of the Historian's work is precisely to demonstrate how much we need the inspired interpreter who sees more clearly than his contemporaries the often invisible hand of God in such earthly affairs. In a profound sense, the Historian has taught us that God has redeemed that seemingly meaningless collection of monotonous moments which we call history. In the same way the Gospel writers and the apostle Paul taught us through their works that God was, in a very ordinary time, reconciling the world to himself through a Galilean.

1 SAMUEL

Samuel, the Last Judge
1:1 to 7:17

The Birth of Samuel (1:1 to 2:11)

The story of Israel's greatest period of advance begins with a birth, and it well should, for God's use of human personality is shown throughout these pages. The book of Samuel is a book about men whom God touched . . . and how they lived out their lives after experiencing his touch. Small wonder the Gospel writers sensed a similarity between the life of Jesus and that of Samuel (compare 2:26 with Luke 2:52).

Elkanah, Hannah, and Peninnah (1:1-2).—The story opens on a note of anguish. Hannah (Grace) had no children. Barrenness deprived a woman like Hannah of far more than the joy of having a child. It robbed her of her sense of worth and dignity, for women were expected to bear children for their husbands. The husband in this case was a man named Elkanah whose hometown was one of the Ramahs north of Jerusalem, in the territory of Ephraim. Hannah's situation was made even more demeaning because of the other woman in the household who had borne children to Elkanah. Her name was Peninnah (Pearl). The Old Testament assumed that such a family arrangement was permissible (Deut. 21:15; Gen. 16:3; 29:31ff).

The way it was (1:3-8).—Looking back across the years, the author described a scene repeated annually when the family of Elkanah journeyed to Shiloh, a great sanctuary city not far from Ramah. Three new characters appear here, Eli and his two sons, Hophni and Phinehas. They served as priests at Shiloh. Peninnah, surrounded by sons and daughters, rubbed it in! Apparently the trip to the house of the Lord was the most painful event of the year for Hannah, for it meant participating in the worship of him whom she believed had "closed her womb" (1:5). Worship is not pleasant when one believes that God is an enemy! The situation was made even more unbearable by the ritual involved. Sacrifices were not just burned on the altar; some were divided among the worshipers (1:5).

But Peninnah's family got the lion's share of the feast. A footnote to verse 5 in the *Revised Standard Version* lists this verse as "obscure." This translation stresses that Hannah got only one portion. Other translations suggest that Elkanah gave her a special portion. Either meaning is possible, though the latter seems more likely.

Regardless of the quantity involved, Hannah refused to partake (1:7). The tension must have mounted each year as the drama built toward this climax. Elkanah's frustration is that of a man who has done all in his power to help, only to be faced with an "unreasonable" response (1:8). Elkanah asserted that the love and consideration Hannah received from him was better than the treatment she could have earned by having ten sons. Elkanah's assertion may well explain why Peninnah taunted Hannah. Hannah received more affection and consideration than Peninnah although she got fewer portions of the public sacrifice. Perhaps Peninnah deserves our sympathy, too!

Hannah's vow (1:9-11).—Apparently the eating of the sacrifice was done apart from the Temple itself. Hannah went to the Temple where Eli was on duty at the entrance (1:9). Within sight of Eli, whether inside the Temple or in front of it is not clear, Hannah prayed at length with great emotion. The bulk of her prayer is not summarized here, but her vow is. A vow involved a promise of a gift to God if he intervened to help (see Gen. 28:20; Ps. 56:12; 116:14,18). Since a vow usually involved the risk of a significant sum of money or a valued animal, it was not to be offered lightly (Eccl. 5:4-5). The animal was a family possession; thus, a woman could not unilaterally make a vow, at least during some periods of Israel's history. The husband or father held veto power over a woman's vow (Num. 30:1-15). In this instance Hannah vowed to dedicate any son she bore to God's service, asserting that she would not allow his hair to be cut. Long hair was a sign both of the warrior and the Nazirite (Num. 6:5; Judg. 13:5).

Eli's blessing (1:12-18).—Eli's first impression of Hannah was grossly false. A better warning against making premature judgments could hardly be imagined. (But note Abraham's confession, Gen. 20:11.) Eli presumed that Hannah was drunk. Perhaps this indicates that many people who "worshiped" were drunk. Ancient festivals were not solemn and sedate affairs (Judg. 21:19-24). Hannah protested her innocence, denying that she was a "base woman" (literally, a daughter of Belial; see Judg. 19:22 and 1 Sam. 2:12 where a similar phrase is involved). Although Hannah's denial of drunkenness contains stereotyped language, it may be intended to suggest that she was fit to bear and dedicate such a child because she kept the Nazirite law herself (Judg. 13:14). Eli's response was to join her in prayer that God would grant her request and give her his blessing (1:17). This was enough to transform Hannah's attitude (1:18).

The divine intervention (1:19-20).—Upon returning home to Ramah, "in due time" (1:20) Hannah became pregnant. Clearly, the writer believed this to be the result of God's action—the Lord remembered and did as she requested (1:11)—yet his action was in and through the human birth process (1:19). For the phrase "knew his wife," see Genesis 4:17. Scholars puzzle over the explanation of Samuel's name. The name "Samuel" is made up of the Hebrew words for "name" and "God," but the name is explained as though it came from the Hebrew word "to ask," which sounds much more like the name Saul than the name Samuel. The explanation fits the situation but does not explain the composition of the name.

The vow fulfilled (1:21-28).—Hannah did not return with the family for the next yearly festival and perhaps not for the next two festivals. Elkanah went "to pay his vow" (1:21). Apparently he, too, had pledged something to God and prayed for Hannah. Hannah delayed returning to the Temple until she could fulfill her vow of giving her son to the Lord. This demanded time to wean the child. When Hannah took her child she also took a significant offering, a three-year-old bull plus flour and wine (or three bulls, as the footnote indicates). These were not meant to substitute for the child but to complete the vow with thanksgiving. If Hannah returned home and left the baby she had so wanted, one can hardly describe the pathos of the scene. But note that 2:11 says that Elkanah went home and does not mention Hannah. Perhaps she stayed to make the transition easier; but ultimately she fulfilled her vow. Her vow brought her peace of mind (1:18), but it demanded a great sacrifice of her. The word for "lent" (1:28) is a form of the same word used to explain Samuel's name.

Hannah's prayer (2:1-11).—Hannah's prayer is like a hymn which a worshiper might sing at the Temple. It is used here to express the awe that Hannah felt. Later many of these same words found their way into Mary's song (Luke 1:46-56). As is often the case when a

worshiper uses a hymn sung by millions, some of the lines do not fit
the situation of the individual. In this case, the phrase, "The barren
hath born seven" (2:5), expresses the truth that a barren woman has
given birth but does not fit Hannah's exact situation. The author
may have used a psalm from his own hymnal to express Hannah's
feelings. If so this would explain the reference to a king (2:10). Israel
had no king until after Hannah's time.

Hannah's prayer first describes God (2:1-8) and then expresses
confidence that he will defeat the enemies through the king (2:9-10).
The bulk of the description focuses on God's reversal of the roles of
the weak and the strong (v. 4), the full and the hungry (v. 5), the
barren woman and the mother (v. 5), and the rich and the poor (vv.
7-8). Wherever arrogant power oppresses the helpless, the Lord who
created the earth (v. 8) and has the power of life and death (v. 6) and
is holy (v. 2) weighs the action (v. 3). This Lord will ultimately intervene, asserts the psalmist, through his chosen king (vv. 9-10).

In Hannah's case God had reversed the roles of the two wives—at
least he had given Hannah reason to exult (v. 1). Samuel, and perhaps Hannah, remained in Shiloh (2:11).

Samuel and the House of Eli (2:12-36)

The center of attention now turns to the negative side of the
events. The situation that called for divine intervention intertwines
with glimpses of the child Samuel and his family whom God blessed.

The sin of Eli's house (2:12-17).—Ironically, Eli's sons are characterized with the same derogatory word used by Eli concerning
Hannah. They were "sons of Belial," worthless men (2:12). Literally,
the text says that they did not know the Lord (v. 12). Their lack of
regard for God was evident in the way they treated their office.
Although the law prescribed specific parts of an animal as the priest's
due, they insisted on the right to take whatever they wished (vv.
13-14) whenever they desired (vv. 15-16). The fat portions were
especially sacred (Lev. 3:16), but these priests ignored the very dis-
tinctions it was their duty to preserve.

Samuel and his family (2:18-21).—As a child Samuel ministered
under Eli's supervision (2:11,18). Perhaps the Lukan account of
Jesus in the Temple at age twelve (Luke 2:41-51) reflects this verse

and shows Jesus as greater than Samuel. Although the ephod cannot be described exactly, it obviously designated its wearer as a priest (Ex. 28:4-14; Judg. 8:27). Contrary to Eli's sons, Samuel's parents were models of devotion. Hannah saw her son annually and brought him a new robe each year. The story hints at the difference in Hannah's attitude during these years. Her burden had been removed. In subsequent years Hannah bore five more children (2:21). Eli's blessing referred each year to the vow in which Hannah "asked" for a child (1:20) and "lent" him to God. Both words are the same and reflect the meaning of Samuel's name. During those years, Samuel "grew"; literally, he "became great" with the Lord (2:21).

Eli and his sons (2:22-25).—A new charge against Eli's sons emerges in this section, and the charges were made not by anonymous worshipers but by Eli himself. The charge was of sexual misconduct with women Temple personnel (v. 22). Eli treated this sin as a sin "against the Lord," as distinct from a wrong committed against a person (2:25). This view of sin assumes the understanding of God of that day but not of the later Christian era. It also assumes that ritual sins or sins related to the priestly service are graver than sins of an interpersonal nature. Jesus altered this ancient perspective. The sons refused to listen (v. 25). The biblical interpreter concluded that such obstinate behavior would lead to their death, and that God willed that they die (2:25). Compare 1 Chronicles 10:14 and the description of Saul's actual death (1 Chron. 10:4).

Samuel's status (2:26).—The alternation of scenes continues to highlight the increasing distance between Samuel and Eli's sons. This is the third reference to Samuel's growing status (2:11,21,26).

A prophetic condemnation of Eli's house (2:27-36).—These verses form one long prophetic sermon introduced by the well-known "Thus the Lord has said" (2:27). It includes a summary of the charge against Eli (v. 29) and beginning with the "therefore" (v. 30), the announcement of judgment. Both were spoken by an unnamed prophet (v. 27). Recalling the age-old story of Moses and Aaron, the prophet listed three duties of a priest: offering sacrifice at the altar, assisting in prayer by burning incense, and determining the will of God by means of the ephod (v. 28). Their needs had been provided for by the statute, but Eli had allowed his sons to make a mockery of their duties. Thus the prophet announced the Lord's intention to revoke the earlier divine covenant with the family of Aaron, at least as it was continued through Eli's descendants. Eli's two sons were to die without replacement (v. 32). Others who would be left would experience desperate circumstances because they would be cut off from their priestly livelihood.

Moreover, this judgment would produce a positive result. A "faithful priest" would replace Eli. It would seem that Samuel's lineage would be intended except for the description of this priest as serving "My anointed," that is, "My king." Since this seems to refer to David's line, it is possible that the Historian leaped over Samuel's era and noted a new line of priests who emerged in David's time, the descendants of Zadok. In this regard, compare 1 Kings 13.

Samuel's Call (3:1 to 4:1a)

On recognizing the call of God (3:1-9).—Again the Historian provides a radar-like glimpse of Samuel's progress: he is ministering under Eli's guidance. Even more significant was the fact that God seldom had anyone to speak through. The terms "word of the Lord" and "vision" (v. 1) refer to prophetic activity. Compare Proverbs 29:18 where the word *vision* is translated as "prophecy." Without divine direction society strays off course. Perhaps this sad fact pointed an accusing finger at the quality of people available. But it may also show why Samuel did not immediately recognize God's call—it was a rare experience!

Eli was old (ninety-eight, according to 4:15) and blind, or nearly so (3:2). Apparently Eli lived in a room adjacent to the sanctuary, and Samuel actually slept in the Temple itself. The ark of God (v. 3) was the sacred object which originated in the wilderness period (Ex. 25:10) and led the people into the Promised Land (Josh. 3:6). In the period of the judges the ark was kept at Bethel where the people would "inquire" before the ark (Judg. 20:27). Thus Samuel slept at the spot where people expected God to speak!

That the lamp of God had not gone out may indicate that the time of day was early morning (Ex. 27:20; 30:7-8). But since the lamp in the sanctuary was supposed to burn continually, and not just during the night, the statement may mean that because of Samuel's ministry, there was still a divine presence in Israel. (See also a similar statement concerning David; 1 Kings 15:4).

At this point Samuel did not "know the Lord" (v. 7). The same words are applied to Hophni and Phinehas (2:12) but are translated with quite a different meaning. The difference seems to be that in Samuel's case he did not yet have the experience of receiving God's word. Hophni and Phinehas could not receive it because of their character. Thus when God called, Samuel did not recognize that he was hearing the divine word. Three times God called, and each time the boy responded *to Eli.* Eli finally understood the meaning of the event and helped shape Samuel's response (v. 9). One wonders in the light of the subsequent account whether this rare occurrence caused joy or fear to rise up in the old priest.

The message of Eli (3:10-14).—This passage delivers a second pronouncement of judgment to Eli. (See 2:30-36.) The fourth time the Lord called, Samuel responded as Eli instructed him. The message he received began with an appraisal of the effect the words would have: ears would tingle (v. 11). God's action would be dramatic. He announced an end to the priestly house of Eli because Eli did not prevent the evil behavior of his sons. It may be noted that this was not simply a matter of the misbehavior of children but the failure of a priest to supervise the Temple. The sin of the priests involved "blaspheming God" (v. 13). This word means dishonoring God or treating God lightly. Following this indictment the sentence was handed down: the sin would never be atoned. (See Lev. 16:6 for atoning by a sacrifice.) It is interesting to note that this sin was committed by professional religious office-holders and involved an arrogant and flagrant violation of sacred duties! It was not merely a moral slip. Abiathar's banishment many years later (1 Kings 2:27) fulfills one or both of the judgments against Eli. But one of Eli's descendants still served as David's priest five generations later (2 Sam. 8:17).

Receiving a hard word (3:15-18).—Eli demanded to know the content of the vision. Perhaps he could tell by Samuel's reluctance to talk that the message would be hard for him to hear (v. 15). Eli invoked an oath to buttress his demand (v. 17). This phrase had become a standardized oath, but it assumed that one would think of a sacrificial animal sliced in two (Gen. 15:10) as the oath was pronounced: "May God do so to you." Upon hearing the content of the vision, Eli responded with an air of acceptance, showing no hostility and offering no excuses.

Samuel, the prophet (3:19 to 4:1a).—This is the final summary of Samuel's progress. (See 2:11,21,26; 3:1,7.) Samuel's word became the word of the Lord for all Israel (4:1a). His pronouncements were always right; the Lord upheld his word (v. 19). Thus Samuel was known from Dan in the north to Beer-sheba in the south as a prophet. In actuality Samuel's activity seemed to be confined to the northern hill country, though his reputation advanced far and wide.

Philistines and the Ark (4:1b-22)

The loss of the ark is told in scenes which swing back and forth between the Israelite and Philistine camps. Scene one describes the dismay in the Israelite camp over their defeat (vv. 1b-4). Scene two lets us see the consternation in the Philistine camp when the ark arrived (vv. 5-10). The second battle is recorded tersely (vv. 10-11), and the succeeding scenes alternate between two people who receive the disastrous news, Eli (vv. 12-18) and the wife of Phinehas (vv. 19-22).

The first defeat (4:1b-4).—The first of these scenes begins in the middle of verse 1. Philistines were newcomers to the land of Canaan like the Israelites. They arrived along the seacoast shortly before the Israelites arrived in the hills. The struggle for the land between these two peoples was fierce—and the Philistines came off better in the early going. There were only five major Philistine cities, each with its own ruler. But these cities fought together. They also had weapons of iron which Israel did not have (1 Sam. 13:19-21). New technology gave distinct advantages then as now!

The battle scene was situated on the coastal plain. Aphek is identifiable, but Ebenezer has not been located (see 7:12). The Historian wastes no words on the battle itself. Obviously his major interest lay elsewhere. He turned immediately to the scene after the battle. It is common in the Old Testament to blame the Lord for defeats (Ps. 89:38). Thus the questions that followed a military defeat, at least in retrospect, were theological, not military (4:3). If God fought against them, they needed to know why. Since God spoke from the ark (3:10), the people decided to bring God into the camp with them (v. 3). Salvation here is thought of in physical terms.

Hophni and Phinehas brought the "ark of the covenant of the

Lord of hosts who is enthroned on the cherubim" (4:4) from Shiloh to the battlefield. Saul later did the same (14:18). The phrase "enthroned on the cherubim" refers to the shape of the ark. The cherubim were fashioned as winged beings at each end of the chest (Ex. 25:20). As if worshiping someone in the center, the cherubim extended their wings inward and bowed. Ancient Israel thought of God as enthroned—seated or standing—above the cherubim wings: thus the name used here. (But see also 1 Kings 6:23-27 for a different understanding of the cherubim.)

The coming of the ark (4:5-9).—The Historian gave only one line to the Israelites' bringing in of the ark. The remainder of the verses tell the story from the perspective of the Philistine camp. Perhaps Numbers 10:35-36 helps explain "the mighty shout" (v. 5) raised by Israel. It was a ritual greeting of the ark as well as the joyous shout of people greeting their deliverer. Note also the shout that accompanied the ark in battle in Joshua's victory at Jericho (Josh. 6:8-11,16,26). Obviously, the great noise meant something; the Philistines needed to learn what it was (v. 6). How they learned about the ark is not recorded, but they concluded that one of the Israelite gods had arrived (v. 7). The Philistines were polytheists and assumed the same of Israel. But Israel also treated the ark, which represented God, as if it meant that God himself were present (v. 3; "that he may come").

The Philistines reacted with despair: "Woe to us" (see Isa. 6:5). Considering themselves already captured, they wailed, "Who shall deliver us?" (v. 8). The word translated "power" literally means "hand"; so the Philistines asked who could snatch them out of the hand of Israel's "gods." Deliverance from the hand of the enemy is a major theme in the Old Testament (Judg. 2:16; Ex. 18:10; Josh. 24:10; and many other examples). The Philistine cry is the ancient equivalent to the cry of the Philippian jailor, "What must I do to be saved?" (Acts 16:30).

The Philistines testified in their despair to the delivering power of Israel's Lord "who smote the Egyptians" (v. 8). Then the speaker changed. A leader challenged and inspired his soldiers not to let Israel turn the tables on them (see Judg. 14:4). Apparently he was an effective speaker.

The second defeat (4:10-11).—Again the historian reported the event itself without elaboration, as though he were hurrying through a long story to reach his point. Contrary to the hopes raised by the coming of the ark, Israel lost the battle. Worse still, the ark was lost to the Philistines. And among the thousands slain only two mattered to the author: Hophni and Phinehas were dead.

The news reached Eli (4:12-18).—The news of Israel's defeat reached Shiloh through a messenger. As in the preceding scene, there is a commotion followed by a question about its meaning and the action resulting from learning what has happened. Attention still centered on Eli and the ark. Eli's "heart trembled for the ark of God" (v. 13), and when he heard of its capture he collapsed (v. 18). Condemned for his administration of the Temple, very old and blind, Eli still had his heart centered around the ark which he had kept for a lifetime. It was news of its loss rather than word of his own sons' deaths that sent him to his grave (v. 18). The Historian noted that Eli was an old man and "heavy." The Hebrew word for "heavy" also means "weighty" or "honored." It seems likely that the Historian intended to note that this person who served so long was an elder and an honored figure. He was not commenting on his size.

The birth of Ichabod (4:19-22).—The news of the ark's loss reached the unnamed wife of Phinehas along with news of her husband's death. This traumatic experience sent her into labor, and she delivered a son. Unlike Hannah, this woman's grief was not lessened by the birth; the joyous announcement was muted by the sad news of death and defeat. Her response to the news of her personal loss and Israel's national tragedy was that "glory is departed from Israel" (v. 21). This is the exact opposite of the statement in Luke that "the glory of the Lord shone around" the shepherds. It signaled the presence of God (Luke 2:9). Israel had suffered the loss of God both on the battlefield and in the loss of the ark.

The Journey of the Ark (5:1 to 7:1)

The account of the ark's journey through the Philistine cities and back to Israelite territory tells a double story. It speaks of the sovereignty of the God who can't be "captured" on the one hand. But on the other, it hints that the ark was moving toward its special place and could not be stopped short, either in Philistia or in Bethshemesh or in Kirjath-jearim. Ultimately it would arrive in Jerusalem (2 Sam. 6:1ff).

The ark in Ashdod (5:1-7).—Ashdod was one of five Philistine cities. Thanks to the work of archaeologists, its ancient site by the sea can once again be visited. The "house of Dagon" apparently refers to a temple dedicated to the god of grain ("Dagon" in Hebrew). The story—as told, it must be remembered, by an Israelite—portrays Dagon as a god who simply couldn't stand before the Lord. On successive mornings his statue fell over; the second time the statue's head and hands broke off. The point of the story is summed up well by the men of Bethshemesh a little later, "Who is able to stand before the Lord, this holy God?" (6:20; Ps. 24:3). Even Israelites found it dangerous to stand in the presence of God! In contrast to the severed hands of Dagon, "the hand of the Lord" worked mightily against Ashdod, afflicting it as if it were Egypt of old. The word "tumors" literally means "swellings" or "hills."

The journey of the ark through Philistia (5:8-12).—Only two other cities of the Philistines, Gath and Ekron, actually needed the ark. The citizens of Ekron refused to keep it, suggesting that it be returned to "its own place" (v. 11). Although a reader might suppose that "its place" would have been Shiloh, this is clearly not what is meant. Second Samuel 6:17 tells of the end of the ark's journey from the house of Eli to the house of David and notes that David set it "in its place" in Jerusalem! The accusing cry of Ekron that the ark was sent "to slay us" (v. 10) sounds much like the murmuring of Israel in the wilderness (Ex. 16:3).

Returning the ark (6:1-9).—Such a dangerous object as the ark had to be treated carefully, so the Philistines posed a series of questions to the priests (of Dagon?) and diviners who could interpret signs. To the first question the answer apparently was, "Send the ark back!" The second question involved protocol. What had to accompany the ark to bring relief from the plague God had sent (v. 2)? The Philistine priests answered as if they were Hebrews; to bring healing a guilt offering had to accompany the ark (Lev. 5). The next question asked what a proper guilt offering would be (v. 4), and the answer introduces a new element into the story. The guilt offering involved replicas of both the "tumors" and the mice. Mice had not been mentioned earlier. It is possible that, like the story of the plagues on Egypt, there were originally at least two separate episodes of punishment. Or perhaps the mice played an unmentioned part in bringing the tumors. In either case, the belief that such offerings needed to resemble that which they were meant to affect (v. 5) ran deep in Israelite faith (Num. 21:8).

The link with the Egyptian plagues becomes obvious in verse 6. The priests—again speaking as if they were Israelites—reminded their people of the end result of the Egyptian episodes. Since ultimately Egypt had to let Israel go, why bring all ten plagues about before acting? At this point the Philistine priests finally answered the first question asked (v. 2): the ark was to be sent back in such a way that the questions of its role in the disastrous events could be answered. These ancient people wrestled with the question of history, too. Was God really at work in the affairs of men? Or were the disasters and the presence of the ark merely coincidentally related? Like the Israelites, the Philistines believed that carefully observed events could interpret the meaning of history (Isa. 7:14-17). In this case the sign was to be the behavior of a new cart and a team of cows that had never pulled a cart before and whose natural instincts would be to find their calves. If the cows acted contrary to the expected, it would be assumed that a power beyond them was causing their behavior (v. 9). If the cows went toward Bethshemesh, an Israelite town, instead of returning to Philistine territory, the priests and diviners would conclude that the Israelite God was responsible for the plagues.

The ark arrives in Israel (6:10-16).—The cart carrying the ark and the guilt offerings moved directly to Bethshemesh, confirming the suspicions of the Philistines that the Lord had been directing the events in their land all along. The ark arrived at a spot that Israel could later point to—a field that had a large stone in it (v. 14). The owner of the field became famous because a great event happened in his field.

The Israelites received the ark with just as much concern for correct procedure as the Philistines who sent it away. Levites alone handled the ark (v. 15; 1 Chron. 15:2). The people kept neither the cows nor the cart but immediately offered them up to God (v. 14). The burnt offering mentioned here involved the burning of the complete animal (Lev. 1) as opposed to the sacrifice mentioned earlier in which only the fat was burned (2:15) and the rest eaten by priests and worshipers. The episode closes with the departure of the Philistines (v. 16).

A summary (6:17-18).—Since only three Philistine cities were mentioned earlier, the historian added a summary note to explain why there were five images. Each of the five cities were represented. But whereas only five mice were mentioned earlier (6:4), this summary suggests that there were golden mice not only for the five major cities but for "all the cities" controlled by the five lords (v. 18).

The ark among the Israelites (6:19 to 7:1).—The story changes abruptly! The ark also brought disaster upon Bethshemesh! The text is not crystal clear on what happened and at best gives only a glimpse of the event. The men of Bethshemesh apparently did not preserve the proper distance between themselves and the holy God. Whether they "looked into" the ark (v. 19) and thus got very close, or merely "looked at" the ark in some improper way, cannot be determined. The Hebrew text may mean either. The people of Bethshemesh suffered a disastrous loss of either seventy men or fifty thousand. They attributed the disaster to divine judgment for their own improper behavior. The Israelites asked the same kind of questions the Philistines had asked. Presumably the questions were answered by local priests, perhaps by casting lots between several nearby cities (v. 20). After determining that Kiriath-jearim should receive the ark—and without mentioning what had happened to them—Bethshemesh sent word to their neighboring city to come get the ark. Kiriath-jearim was midway to Jerusalem, but it was also on the way to Shiloh which was north of Jerusalem. In Kiriath-jearim the ark was placed in Abinadab's home, and his son Eleazar was ordained to care for it. Samuel no longer served at the ark, and for the next generation or more the ark occupied its "temporary" home (7:2).

The Ministry of Samuel (7:2-17)

After a long interval in the story Samuel reappears here. He is no longer at Shiloh and, apparently, he is twenty years older (v. 2). Nothing is known of the intervening years. Samuel still serves in a priestly role, but he is called a "judge."

Samuel calls for rededication (7:3-4).—When Israel lamented (v.

2), she cried out to God because of some distress. Many of the psalms are laments (Ps. 44:9-12). The military picture had grown worse instead of better since the ark had come back.

As the text picks up the scene, Samuel delivered a challenge to the people to prove their seriousness by putting away the other deities sometimes worshiped. (Compare Amos 4:6-12; note the phrase, "Yet you did not return to me.") Baals and Ashtaroth were the male and female gods worshiped by the Canaanites. Obviously Canaanite religion had "conquered" Israel even though Israel captured the land. Perhaps this call to rededication was part of an annual ritual of covenant renewal. Spiritual rededication was viewed by the Historian as a prerequisite for military victory.

Defeat of the Philistines (7:5-11).—Mizpah, which lies a few miles north of Jerusalem, was one of three cities where Samuel served regularly (7:16). At Mizpah Samuel led the people in a sacrificial service which was part of the process of lamenting. Nowhere else in the Old Testament is water poured out as a sacrifice (v. 6). The liquid offerings usually involved wine (Lev. 23:13) or blood (Lev. 4:7), although Elijah had water poured on his sacrifice (1 Kings 18:33). In New Testament times the ritual of the Feast of Tabernacles involved pouring water as a reminder of God's provision of water in the wilderness (Num. 20:2-13; John 7:37-39). The people urged Samuel to cry out for them (v. 8), that is, to lead in expressing their distress and in calling for God's help (Ps. 77:1). Samuel offered a young lamb as a sacrifice and "cried to the Lord," and the Lord "answered" (v. 9). Those technical terms appear again in the coming chapters and play a significant role in the story (8:18; 14:37ff; 28:6). In this instance the "answer" seems to have been the rumble of thunder which routed the Philistines (v. 10). Thus all Israel had to do was pursue a fleeing enemy, because God had fought for them. The Historian presents much of his story in this manner, relating victory and defeat to spiritual faithfulness.

The end of the war (7:12-14).—The setting up of a commemorative stone must have been a common occurrence in ancient times. Like modern newspaper accounts or historical books, they served as records of events. The word *Ebenezer* is a combination of two Hebrew words meaning "stone" and "help." Since it is clear from the rest of the story that the Philistines continued to threaten Israel's very survival, verse 13 must mean that in Samuel's time the Philistines did not mount another attack. The cities recovered are not named but were probably places which lay in the border between the two lands, where the foothills of Judah meet the plain. The Amorites were the original Canaanite population.

Samuel's ministry (7:15-17).—Samuel "judged" Israel in three cities. Bethel and Mizpah are in the central highlands north of Jerusalem. Gilgal was somewhere in the Jordan Valley, if this is the same city where Joshua first entered the Land (Josh. 4:19). Samuel made his home at Ramah, probably the same as the city of his parents, Elkanah and Hannah (1:1); it was not far from Mizpah. The phrase "he administered justice" is a translation of the word "judged" (v. 17); the same verb is used in verse 15.

Saul, the First King
8:1 to 15:35

The Request for a King (8:1-22)

The prophet Hosea once spoke of a prophet who "preserved" Israel (Hos. 12:13). One wonders if he spoke of Samuel. These chapters tell the story of the transition from the leadership of priests (like Eli) and judges (like Samuel) to a centralized kingship under Saul. First steps are faltering ones, and Israel's first step into a monarchy was no exception. With the skill of a master, the Historian portrayed the flowering and failing of this first effort. He linked the process unforgettably to the relationship between Samuel and Saul. By the story's end it is difficult to know for whom to weep—aging Samuel, doomed like Moses never to enter the Land to which he had led his people, or a praying Saul who heard no word from God (28:6) and only hard words from his pastor.

An ominous repetition (8:1-3).—The second generation failed again. Whereas Eli's sons treated their inherited priesthood with contempt (2:1), Samuel's sons corrupted the role of the judge (but see 1 Chron. 6:33). Beersheba, if this name refers to the well-known city in the south, was the last city before the forbidding desert. Were Samuel's sons sent there to hold the frontier or to remove them from

the nation's center? Their moral failure convinced Israel's leaders
that they could not succeed their father. The introduction of kingship results from the failure of men to honor their offices.

The request for a king (8:4-9).—Throughout the next few chapters
negative and positive statements about kingship intertwine. In some
cases it is not easy to tell on which side of the balance to place a
verse. When the elders requested a king "to govern us like all the
nations," the tone may be positive (see Deut. 17:14). But Samuel
interpreted the request as a personal rejection. The Historian wrote
that the Lord considered the request as rejection of his kingship (v.
7), like Israel's earlier reversion to the golden calf (v. 8; Ex. 32).
Clearly, the Historian remembered this episode as a sinful moment
in Israel's past.

The ways of a king (8:10-18).—Samuel proceeded to describe the
rights which kings assumed. He dealt with the subject under several
headings: sons (v. 11); daughters (v. 13); fields, vineyards, and
orchards (vv. 14-15); male and female slaves (v. 16); and animals
(vv. 16-17). In each case Samuel declared that a king could appropriate either the best or a part of each category for himself. Other
passages reflect the truth of his words (Amos 7:1; 1 Kings 4:22).
Samuel warned that in the future Israel's kings would cause her to
"cry out" just as her enemies had (v. 18; 7:8), but that God would
not "answer" (Hos. 13:9-11). They could not expect God to ease the
burden they chose to carry.

The reaffirmation of the demand (8:19-22).—While the language
of these verses sounds completely negative, it may not in fact be so.
The "no" of the people (v. 19) is remarkably like that of Israel when
she responded to Joshua (Josh. 24:21). In that case the "no" meant,
"Joshua, you can't scare us out of worshiping the Lord. We will serve
him whatever the cost!" Here too a similar ritual is involved. The
leader tests the resolve of the people by picturing a hard road ahead,
but the people refuse to be turned aside. The Historian recorded that
the Lord himself commanded his aging and reluctant spokesman to
honor the commitment (vv. 21-22). Thus an originally positive account of the choice of a king involving a ritual of rededication
appears now more negative than it may have been. Samuel's command that each person return to his city may have prepared the way
for a crowning of the king in *each* of the three cities Samuel served,
Bethel, Gilgal, and Mizpah. Stories related to at least two of these
follow.

The Anointing of Saul (9:1 to 10:16)

The preceding chapter described the origin of kingship in Israel as a rejection of God (8:7) which ultimately would cause the nation grief (8:18). Even so the Historian pictured God as gently urging the elderly judge to "make them a king" (8:22). There seem to be several versions of what happened next. Perhaps there was more than one ceremony crowning Saul. The famous story of the young man who set out looking for lost asses and found a kingdom stresses the positive involvement of God in the process. Subsequent accounts present a more negative description.

Introducing Saul (9:1-2).—Benjamin is the territory just north of Jerusalem. Kish, Saul's father, was a wealthy farmer. Saul was both taller and handsomer than most, and he was young. Just how old Saul was is unknown (see 13:1). His size and looks indicated to the people that he was favored by God.

The search (9:3-4).—Saul and his servant left Gibeah, where Saul's home is said to have been (11:4). Their itinerary can't be traced. Ephraim was the territory in the middle of Canaan, north of Judah and Benjamin. Shalisha may be the same as Baalshalisha (2 Kings 4:42), which was associated with Gilgal, one of Samuel's cities. Shaalim is unknown. The journey probably did not involve many miles distance from home.

The decision (9:5-10).—The land of Zuph was Samuel's home territory, as indicated by the "zophim" in the name of Elkanah's city (1:1). The seemingly random wanderings led Saul directly to the one spot where he needed to be. Moreover, Saul's servant knew about the "man of God" there (v. 6). He described Samuel just as the Historian had pictured him earlier (3:19), as one whose word could be trusted. When Saul hesitated because he had no money to give the prophet, the servant again took charge and offered to pay what he had—though it may not have been much. Verse 9 is in parentheses to indicate that it is an editorial note. It seems to explain the word "seer" which first appears in verse 11; thus it is a little out of place. This verse indicates that the terminology of prophecy changed in Israel. The word "seer" once meant the same thing as prophet. In fact, prophets are frequently described as "seeing" (Isa. 6:1; Jer. 1:11). The parenthetical note explains why one would go to a "man of God" to find lost asses. When these words were written prophets did not fill such a role.

The ascent (9:11-14).—The city sat on a hill. In most cases the approach to a city would have been a curving road that ascended around the hill. This city's well was at the foot of the hill, and maidens had the chore of carrying water up the steep hill. From some of these girls Saul learned that the "seer" was in the city for a sacrifice at the high place (v. 12). The high place may have been situated on the highest spot in the area, but the term could be applied to a worship site in general. Samuel's presence was required to "bless" the sacrificial meal (v. 13; see also 13:8-9).

The revelation (9:15-17).—The Historian turned the clock back to show what had happened a day earlier. Samuel received a word from the Lord that he was to anoint a Benjamite as prince the following day (v. 16). Anointing was the ancient ritual of consecration that involved either pouring or smearing oil on a person or an object. Priests, sacred stones, the tabernacle, and kings—among others—were anointed. Ultimately the term *anointed* became a technical term for God's chosen ruler. Samuel was to designate Saul as "prince" (v. 16). This term does not mean heir to the throne. It is a synonym for king (used of David in 13:14; 25:30; of Solomon in 1 Kings 1:35 and others). The new leader's task would be to continue Israel's cry (see 1 Sam. 7:8) for God to hear and save Israel, even as he earlier heard the people in Egypt (Ex. 3:7). Thus kingship here is described as the outcome of God's gracious intervention to save. God revealed to Samuel that Saul was his chosen one (9:17).

The encounter (9:18-21).—The gate of a city was a section of the main road passing through the wall and flanked by massive stone-walled rooms. In times of peace the gate area was the center of life in a city. Saul first met Samuel in such a gate (v. 18). Samuel did not answer Saul's question. Instead he ordered him to the high place and promised to let him leave the next morning (v. 19). The Revised Standard Version translation of verse 19 leaves the impression that Samuel would tell him what he wanted to know "in the morning." But he divulged the information about the lost animals in the next sentence, so perhaps there should have been a period after "I will let you go." By telling Saul about the length of time he had been gone (three days) and the fact that he was looking for his father's lost asses and that they had been found, Samuel was proving his right to command Saul's presence at the sacrifice. The question "for whom is all that is desirable in Israel?" (v. 20) is not clear. Some scholars see in it a hidden reference to Saul's kingship. In the context it seems more likely to be an example of ceremonious hospitality referring to the choice spot reserved for this special guest at the sacrificial meal. Saul responded (v. 21) with equally exaggerated humility that he didn't deserve such treatment, being of the humblest family in his tribe (see 9:1)!

The meal (9:22-24).—The sacrificial meal took place indoors ("the hall") and was attended by about thirty people (v. 22). Saul was given a large portion (perhaps like Hannah in 1:5 and Benjamin in Gen. 43:34), indicating his honored place in the group. The cook indicated that the portion had been reserved in advance (v. 24). By this time the reader knows that the sequence of events was not coincidental. This was the beginning of a bittersweet relationship between prophet and king that dominates the coming chapters.

The anointing (9:25 to 10:1).—The hours following the feast are merely hinted at. Saul spent the night on the flat roof of a house, as was customary. Samuel aroused him early and accompanied Saul and his servant into the empty street. On the edge of town Samuel privately poured oil on Saul's head (2 Kings 9:3) and kissed him. The kiss between men is a common greeting in the semitic world. Then Samuel explained the significance of his act: it was a symbol of what the Lord had done. As the footnote in the Revised Standard Version indicates, the long sentence that follows is absent in the Hebrew texts. However, this verse gives the meaning of what follows. The subsequent events will be signs that Samuel's words were true. Saul has become the prince over the Lord's people, here called his heritage or inheritance (see Eph. 1:18).

The signs (10:2-13).—In the Old Testament a sign need not be a miraculous event in itself. Neither did it have to be immediately apparent. In this instance Samuel gave Saul three signs: in succession he would encounter two men by Rachel's tomb (v. 2), three men going up to Bethel (v. 3), and a group of prophets leaving the high place at Gibeathelohim (v. 5). The fulfillment of all the signs is reported, but only the last is described (v. 10). Nowhere is any hint given of the location of the city where Samuel anointed Saul—except that it was in Zuph (9:5). Three cities were visited regularly by Samuel: Bethel, Gilgal, and Mizpah (7:16). Since Samuel mentions both Bethel (10:3) and Gilgal (v. 8), presumably the anointing took place at Mizpah. Saul was given two signs that were to occur near

Bethel, one at Rachel's tomb (Gen. 35:16) and the other at the oak of
Tabor (Gen. 35:8). The sign consisted in the confirmation that the
lost animals had been found and in the gift of bread (9:7). The third
sign occurred as Saul approached home. Gibeathelohim means "hill
of God." It may be the same as Gibeath, Saul's home. It was the site
of both a Philistine contingency and a high place. There Saul met a
group of prophets. In later years Elijah headed such a group and was
its "father" (2 Kings 2:3-12). The musical instruments mentioned (v.
5) were used to accompany the prophetic ritual which may have involved ecstatic movement and speech. The word "prophesy" itself
probably indicates a frenzied activity. This verb is also translated
"raved" (1 Kings 18:29). The transition from a normal state to that
of a prophetic trance appeared so dramatic that a person was said to
"be turned into another man" (v. 6). Like a powerful figure from the
days of the judges, Saul v.as to seize upon whatever opportunity presented itself to deliver his people (v. 7). Since there is a later reference to a defeat of a garrison of Philistines at Geba (13:3) it is possible that this challenge to seize the opportunity available may originally have referred to a battle with the Philistines (see v. 5).

Verse 8 does not seem to connect with the account of the signs. It
may once have followed immediately upon the anointing of Saul
(10:1) and have been preparatory to an anointing or crowning at
Gilgal where Samuel was headed. A later chapter (13:8) refers to
waiting seven days for Samuel at Gilgal and may be related to this
verse, too.

The fulfillment of Samuel's last sign caused people to talk about
Saul's change (v. 11). This joining of the prophets was obviously not
an isolated experience for Saul (see 19:23-24), and his actions generated a proverb: "Is Saul also among the prophets?" (v. 11). The
proverb reflects surprise that a person of Saul's place in life would be
found with the prophets. The response to the proverb, "And who is
their father?" may also contain a censure of Saul, too (v. 12). It
seems to suggest that the particular prophetic group involved did not
have a respectable leader—they were nobodies! Why did the Historian record the proverbial remarks? The entire account traces the
hand of God in the movement of events leading to this point. Saul
obeyed the prophet, Samuel, explicitly. Yet the people's remarks
were negative. Perhaps it was the Historian's way of commenting on
the fact that the people missed the act of God in their very midsts.

Or, as Jesus said, "A prophet is not without honor, except in his own country. . ." (Mark 6:4).

The secret (10:14-16).—Saul's uncle, who may have been at the high place (v. 13), questioned Saul as if he suspected some unusual motivation for Saul's behavior. But Saul answered each question without revealing the most important thing Samuel said.

The Making of a King (10:17-27)

The Historian has now sketched two quite different scenes, one of a delegation demanding that Samuel make a king (8:4-22) and another of God's imperceptible working in the lives of men to raise up a deliverer for his people. The scene now shifts back to pick up the first thread.

The Mizpah assembly (10:17-19).—Samuel gathered the people together at Mizpah, possibly the site of the meal and the anointing of Saul. Samuel's speech (vv. 18-19) contrasts the deeds of the Lord and the people, "I brought up Israel . . . I delivered you . . . . You . . . rejected . . . ; you have said . . . ." But the indictment does not lead to punishment for the gathered tribes, but, rather, to the fulfillment of their request. Perhaps the explanation of this unusual consequence is that the phrase, " 'No, but set a king over us,' " is intended as a denial of Samuel's interpretation and a solemn reaffirmation of their commitment to a king. (See the treatment of 8:19 above.) If this is true, the tone of the passage is essentially positive.

The choice of Saul (10:20-24).—The process of casting lots involved the use of sacred objects called Urim and Thummim (14:41). By using this means Samuel narrowed the choice between tribes, families, and men within the family. The lot fell on Saul. Because the Historian has already told of Samuel's private choice of Saul, this action seems purely ceremonial. It seems clear that the Historian did not intend to degrade Saul's choice, and it is also clear that his method of alternating scenes may not be intended to produce a chronological account.

The text assumes that the physical presence of all the members of each group was not required for the casting of the lots. Saul was not present when he was selected (v. 21). Using the same sacred objects, they determined that Saul was present and where he was (v. 22).

When the reluctant Saul was finally produced, his physical stature again became obvious (v. 23; 9:2). Repeating this description allowed the historian to tie these two different accounts together. Saul then received the public salute as he had earlier received Samuel's kiss.

The conclusion of the crowning (10:25-27).—Part of the ceremony of inaugurating the king involved depositing a written statement concerning the "rights" of a king "before the Lord" in a sanctuary. The word for "rights" is the same word translated earlier as "ways" (8:11). These words apparently stated what the king was allowed to do, as opposed to Deuteronomy 17:14ff which prohibited the king from excesses. At a later crowning of young Joash the king was given "the testimony" (2 Kings 11:12), which is no longer preserved. After the crowning Saul did not remain in a capital city but returned home with a contingent of brave men. The opposition group are labeled "worthless men," just as the sons of Eli (2:12).

Saul's Heroic Deed (11:1-15)

As in the stories of the judges, God again raised up a deliverer. Saul, like Gideon, was still farming when a crisis presented itself, and he acted in a newfound strength to help his people. As in the case of Gideon (Judg. 8:22), such a heroic deed moved people to accept the leader as a king (11:12).

The scene in Jabesh-gilead (11:1-4).—Gilead and Ammon are territories in Transjordan, on the eastern side of the Jordan River. Gilead is north of Ammon and borders it. The territory of Gilead became a battleground for several generations of Israelites. Jephthah (Judg. 11) fought the Ammonites there over disputed territory. Centuries later King Ahab died trying to recapture Ramoth-gilead from the Syrians who had gained control of it earlier (1 Kings 22). Thus it was not unprecedented for Nahash, whose name means "Snake," to attack an Israelite city in Gilead. A fragment of a Dead Sea Scroll contains some additional verses which describe an earlier stage of this war. The special cruelty of the terms of surrender (v. 2) suggests both the barbarism of warfare even in nonnuclear ages (see also Amos 1:13) and the desperate situation of Jabesh-gilead. The city stalled for time while sending for help (v. 3). It isn't clear whether the messengers came directly to Saul at Gibeah or whether Gibeah was just one of many cities they approached.

Saul's victory (11:5-11).—The Spirit of God came upon Saul. He moved quickly to assume leadership. The sending of pieces of a slain animal constituted both a call to action and an implied threat. Groups that did not respond might be treated like the ox! Saul called the people to follow himself and Samuel (v. 7). Deborah and Barak formed this same kind of alliance between the spiritual and military authorities (Judg. 4:4ff). Saul gathered his army at Bezek between Shechem and Bethshan for the march across the river at Jabesh. The story of the messengers and the sly response of the city with its double meaning (literally, "Tomorrow we will come out to you") would have delighted an Israelite audience. The battle itself is merely reported (v. 11).

The road to kingship (11:12-15).—Unlike Gideon who earlier refused kingship under similar circumstances (Judg. 8:22), Saul accepted the position. Saul overruled his followers who wished to take vengeance on the Israelites who opposed him (vv. 12-13), and Samuel called the people to the sanctuary at Gilgal in the Jordan valley.

Samuel's Sermon to Israel (12:1-25)

This long speech of Samuel continues the ritual of installation begun in the last chapter. Samuel asked for public certification that his own rule was honest and that he had not profited unjustly from public office (vv. 1-5). Next he rehearsed the saving acts of the Lord leading up to the most recent crisis that created the need for a king (vv. 6-13). Finally, he recited the blessings and curses that obedience and disobedience to the Lord could bring (vv. 14-15). The closing episode in the chapter (vv. 16-25) may form part of a different version of this story, or it may be a kind of ritual reaffirmation of intention.

A public accounting (12:1-5).—The changing of the guard from judge to king involved a public auditing of Samuel's reign. Samuel called upon the king, here called "his anointed" (v. 3), and the Lord as witnesses of his integrity. He invited any who could charge him with error to step forth. The list of possible corruption included the illegal taking of animals through fraud, oppression (see Mic. 2:2), or bribery. Oppression involved the use of force; a synonym might be *extortion.* These are the avenues open to men of power for gathering wealth beyond their due. What could be more gratifying to a public official than to come to the final audit knowing that all men would say before God and king that he had taken nothing beyond his due?

Samuel's summary of God's deeds (12:6-13).—Samuel then called upon the people to stand as defendants while he presented his side of the case before the sole witness, the Lord. These included the Exodus from Egypt, the entry into the Promised Land (v. 8), and the history of the subsequent period of the judges. Samuel mentioned specifically three enemies: Sisera (Judg. 4:2), the Philistines (Judg. 3:31), and the king of Moab (Judg. 3:12). He numbered three judges in addition to himself: Jerubbaal or Gideon (Judg. 6—7, or 7:1), Barak (Judg. 4—5), and Jephthah (Judg. 11). The conflict with the Ammonites recounted in chapter 11 is cited here as the direct impetus for changing to a king. Samuel recalled the statement the people made earlier (8:19), reminding them that they had rejected his warning about the ways of a king and reaffirmed their desire for this kind of leader (12:12). At that point, having shown that neither his own acts nor those of the Lord could be faulted, Samuel presented the new king (v. 13). The very words Samuel used echo the name Saul, for Saul's name means "asked for"!

The charge to the nation (12:14-15).—These two verses contain a positive and negative charge, in the style of a treaty between nations. The language used here is similar to that of Deuteronomy, whose ideas dominate the Historian's work. If people and nation fear, serve, obey, and follow the Lord, it will be well (v. 14). The negative charge warned against rebellion against the Lord (literally, "against the mouth of the Lord," v. 15). The saving hand could be expected to turn against those who rebelled.

A final affirmation (12:16-25).—These verses begin again with the demand that the people stand as defendants (as in v. 7). This time a new act of God as opposed to a past act of God was presented. The wheat harvest occurred during late May or June when rain seldom came. Samuel prayed for rain (v. 18), and it came. Samuel presented this as evidence of the "wickedness" done in asking for a king (v. 17). When the people responded as if to withdraw their request out of fear (v. 19), Samuel assured them that, as in days past, if they would serve the Lord, he would not "cast away his people" (v. 22). Samuel also assured the people of his own continued mediation for them (v. 23). The intention of the Historian in this section is debatable. Some feel that he meant to portray kingship as the product of a callous disregard for the Lord's past saving deeds and, therefore, a product of sinful rebellion. The interpretation given here has suggested that the negative elements were largely ritual and may not have been intended to place the institution of kingship itself under condemnation. Quite clearly, the Historian believed that the Lord himself chose David as king and established his throne forever (2 Sam. 7:14)!

Saul's Condemnation (13:1-23)

In this section Saul's kingship begins and ends! Actually, Saul's reign lasted for several years, but the sequence of events is very difficult to sort out. In some ways the account of Saul is like a photograph taken with a telephoto lens; everything seems closer together than it really is. But the story is not just squeezed together, it is also oddly arranged. For example, another story of Samuel's rejection of Saul comes later (15:26), and the present chapter refers to chapter 10 as if nothing came between (note 13:8 and 10:8). Some interpreters assume that duplicate stories have been interwoven to make one account. While there are some undoubted duplications, some of the arrangement may reflect deliberate method. Thus the Historian seems to announce an event and then fill in behind it to show how it came about.

Saul's reign (13:1).—As the Revised Standard Version indicates, the information given is incomplete. The word giving the number of Saul's years is missing. Something also is missing in the next phrase, since Saul's reign seems to have covered a much longer time. (When anointed he was a youth, but he had grown sons fighting with him in his last battle.) Presumably Saul's reign lasted at least twenty-two years, instead of two (see Acts 13:21). We don't know why the numbers were dropped out of the ancient manuscripts.

Saul gathers an army (13:2-4).—Saul selected an army from among those who responded to his call much as Gideon had done earlier. He did not keep all who came (v. 2). Of the three thousand kept, a thousand fought under Jonathan. The names of Gibeah (v. 2) and Geba (v. 3) are very similar. Saul's home was Gibeah, and this is probably where Jonathan was located. Thus the Philistines had a station of soldiers in the very heart of Israelite territory! Jonathan attacked this band of Philistines (see chapter 14). His victory angered the Philistines but served as a rallying point for the Israelites. Saul publicized the victory (v. 3) and called all the people to Gilgal where Israel had gained its first victory upon entering Canaan (Josh. 4:19).

The Philistine threat (13:5-7a).—Although the Historian narrated this description of the Philistines after telling of Israel's victory, he seems to be describing events that occurred earlier. The Philistine buildup at Michmash in the heart of Israel's territory was the threat that caused Saul to gather an army initially. Thus the description of the Hebrews fleeing to the caves, tombs, cisterns, and safer lands reflects not the behavior of Saul's army but the terrible distress of the citizenry. The Philistines were threatening to drive them from their last stronghold. Michmash was southeast of Bethel. (Bethaven means House of Iniquity and was a name applied to Bethel later.)

The scene at Gilgal (13:7b-15a).—The Historian shifted his description back to the Israelite camp at Gilgal. When Samuel anointed Saul he sent him to Gilgal to wait seven days (10:8). The Historian apparently meant to relate this episode to the anointing scene. Saul and the people waited at Gilgal for the prophet/priest Samuel. At two other points in the story the Historian described people as trembling! The elders trembled when Samuel approached Bethlehem, and the priest of Nob trembled when David appeared alone at his door (21:1). In each case the use of this term signals a dangerous turn of events. The people knew that the absence of Samuel meant something full of potential harm. Samuel delayed his coming. Even the army was disintegrating (v. 8). But no action could be taken until the proper sacrifice had been offered. Saul took matters into his own hands—to Samuel this was a critical sign of Saul's little faith—and performed the ritual himself, although he was not a priest. Halfway through the offering (v. 10), Samuel strode into camp. The tension-filled scene, with overtones of God's dialogue with Adam and Eve (Gen. 3:13) and with the guilty Cain (Gen. 4:10), moves swiftly to Samuel's crushing judgment. Because Saul had disobeyed, the Lord had chosen another person. Compare this to man's expulsion from the Garden (Gen. 3:22ff). Saul could have been the person with whom the Lord made an everlasting covenant (v. 13), but he lost this great good as man lost the Garden which he could have kept.

Of men and materials (13:15b-23).—Before the battle actually began Saul's army had shrunk from three thousand to six hundred (v. 15). The Israelites had moved to Geba (but compare 13:2) in the central hills near the Philistine camp at Michmash. Three Philistine units plundered the territory north, west, and east of their camp (v. 18). The point of this note is that the Philistines had a free hand in raiding and looting in the central hills. Verses 19-23 explain further why there was so little resistance. The age of iron had dawned for the more advanced Philistines, but Israel lacked the technology to make and service iron implements. There was no blacksmith in Israel (v. 19). Perhaps the Philistines had prevented Israel from developing such skills. Only the king and his heir had the coveted iron weapons (v. 22). The entire account is a vivid reminder of the terrible price the weak have always paid to the strong and of the role that technology has played in this oppressive system.

Jonathan, Saul, and the War (14:1-52)

Saul emerges in this chapter as a complex man, meticulously pious (v. 24), concerned to obey the command of God (v. 34), utterly sincere (v. 39), but rash (v. 19) and detrimental (v. 29). The Historian has recounted a scene from Saul's kingship that should bring great honor to him. But the negative notes combine with the placement after Saul's rejection to allow this chapter to detract from Saul. Much of the honor belongs to Jonathan; Saul is portrayed as a leader, prone to make mistakes even when attempting to be faithful to the Lord, whom the people must overrule to prevent a massive injustice (v. 45).

The cast of characters (14:1-5).—The spotlight falls on three figures in this episode: Saul, the king; Jonathan, the heroic warrior; and a priest named Ahijah. Saul was still at Gibeah (probably the same as Geba in 13:15). No decisive action had been taken. The fact that Saul's location was under a tree rather than in a palace is

sometimes used as evidence for a "rustic" tone to his kingship, but
this understanding of Saul's reign does not fit the rest of the story.
Here Saul was in the field with his army; no description of his
administration was intended. Ahijah is very carefully described (v.
3) as the continuation of the authentic priesthood of Shiloh associated with both Eli and Samuel. The ephod was a priestly garment
associated with determining God's will (see Ex. 38 and also the
"breastplate of righteousness" in Eph. 6:14). Jonathan, Saul's son, is
the central figure. Here he is described as taking matters into his own
hands without his father's consent. The Philistine camp was located
on an opposing ridge separated from Saul's camp by a rugged
ravine. The names of the two suggest that the terrain was difficult.
"Seneh," that is to say, a thornbush, is essentially the same Hebrew
word as that used for the "bush" that attracted Moses (Ex. 3:2) and
suggests that the area was thickly covered in bush.

Jonathan's feat (14:6-15).—Jonathan's heroic attack resembles
those of the judges who delivered Israel. The battle was God's battle.
It was fought in faith that nothing could prevent his victory (v. 6),
launched after receiving a sign (v. 9), and involved the belief that
victory was "given" by the Lord (v. 12). None of these facts belittles
Jonathan's role. Rather, like David later, he was the Lord's instru-
ment. The Philistines' comment about the Hebrews emerging from
hiding picks up the earlier note that the populace had fled (13:6). In
hand-to-hand combat Jonathan and his armor-bearer prevailed over
twenty Philistines, causing "panic" (literally, "trembling") far
beyond the military base.

Saul's reaction (14:16-23).—At several points in Saul's story,
events forced his hand. Here a king with his army is embarrassed to
see a battle raging about which he knew nothing (v. 16). Assuming
that some of his people were involved, Saul ordered a roll call to find
out who it was. And there he wavered! Saul's first impulse was to
seek God's guidance, so he summoned the priest. The "ark" mentioned here may mean the priestly ephod which contained the sacred
lots. The Bible assumes that the ark itself was taken to Kireath-
jearim and remained there throughout Saul's years (7:2; 2 Sam. 6:2).
But Saul could not wait for Ahijah to complete the process; he had to
go just as earlier he had to start the war before Samuel arrived
(13:8ff). The battle that ensued brought Hebrews out of hiding and

to the side of Saul (14:22) and caused some who had sided with the Philistines to switch back (v. 21). As usual in the Old Testament, both victory and defeat are described as really belonging to God (v. 23).

Saul's rash command (14:24-30).—The scene involved here must be placed back at the beginning of the battle. The Historian frequently has to go back behind a point already described to add details. Apparently Saul commanded the people not to eat as an act of complete dedication to God (v. 24). As Saul's army pursued the enemy they found a forested area with an abundance of honey. Jonathan had been gone (as the earlier section mentioned) when Saul had forbidden food to the people—and he ate (v. 27). When Jonathan was told of his father's command, he criticized his father's decision. The fact that Jonathan thought things could have gone better had the army eaten indicates that there was some failure involved in the campaign.

Saul's altar (14:31-35).—The effects of rigid obedience to God at one point soon led to disobedience elsewhere. The people were so hungry they did not take time to prepare the food according to the law (Lev. 17:3-4). Saul chastised the people and prepared to treat the meat properly. Though the story seems to picture Saul as an exceedingly holy man, it is possible that the Historian was subtly criticizing Saul for once again acting as a priest. At the least he is shown as being the indirect cause of the people's sin.

The effects of Jonathan's "sin" (14:36-46).—When Saul once again consulted the priest for God's will concerning the pursuit of the Philistines, God was silent! This failure to receive an answer prompted a serious search for the sin which prevented God's will from coming. By using the sacred lots called Urim and Thummim (see Ex. 28:30), Saul sought to determine whether the administration or the people were at fault. The phrase "were taken" (v. 41) was a technical term meaning that the lots fell in such a way as to indicate that Saul and Jonathan were guilty. Next the process was repeated to choose between Saul and Jonathan, and the lot fell on Jonathan (v. 42). The process involved here is that of "inquiring" of the Lord. The results could then be presented by the priest as a statement from the Lord (23:2,4). Both Jonathan and Saul accepted the results of the test and were prepared to carry out the penalty (vv. 44-45). But the people were unwilling to allow the person who had saved them to be executed. The people redeemed Jonathan, but the process is not described. And Saul decided not to continue against the Philistines, perhaps concluding that because of Jonathan's breach the victory would not be given to them by the Lord.

A summary of Saul's reign (14:47-52).—The enemies mentioned include those on the eastern border (Moab, Ammon, and Edom), the western border (Philistines) and the northern border (Zobah). The Amalekites were situated to the south. Over all, Saul was given good marks; "he did valiantly" (v. 48). He also built a relatively strong fighting force (v. 52). The people mentioned in verses 49-51 all played a role in the remaining story. Saul's three sons all died with him (see 1 Chron. 8:33 for a difference in names). Saul's two daughters were important in the David story. Abner became a key figure after Saul's death, establishing Saul's surviving son as king and leading his army. Compare 1 Chronicles 8:33 for the relationship of Ner and Kish. Ahinoam, Saul's wife, was mentioned only here, although David later married a different Ahinoam.

Saul's Rejection by Samuel (15:1-35)

Because the Historian had already included one account of Saul's rejection (chap. 13) this account is difficult to place in the flow of events. The enemies here are the Amalekites, not the Philistines. The account opens as if Samuel is anointing Saul king for the first time, and Saul's rejection seems to be a fresh grief for Samuel and not a continuing problem (15:11). Perhaps the Israelites remembered two episodes in which Samuel and Saul clashed. Apparently a prophet's rejection of a king did not remove him from office, for Saul continued to rule until his death. So perhaps it is unnecessary to assume that this account is a "duplicate" of chapter 13. It is impossible to know where this battle should be placed, but since it leads to the final breach between these two giants it apparently came late in Saul's reign.

The prophetic word (15:1-3).—One role of a prophet in Israel was to indicate the Lord's choice of kings. The anointing of Jehu (2 Kings 9:6-7) combines the same elements of announcement and command found here. Thus, this passage may have once told how Saul became king! However, one could understand the opening lines as a reference to a past event that provides the basis for the new command Samuel has to convey. The attack on the Amalekites is not defensive but punitive! The reason lay far in the past when Israel first tried to enter its new land, and Amalek opposed them (Deut. 25:17-19; Ex. 17:8-16). Samuel commanded Saul to place the Amalekites under the ban, that is to sacrifice them to the Lord (v. 3). Needless to say, this concept of war raises profound questions for Christians and is not what Jesus would have condoned. But it was commonplace in Saul's time; both Israel and her enemies practiced such "holy war."

Fulfilling the command (15:4-9).—The battle took place in the southern hills. Since the Amalekites probably were a bedouin clan, their "city" would have been a camp rather than a walled enclosure. The Kenites appear here as kinsmen of Israel to whom kind treatment was due. Moses' father-in-law was a Kenite (Judg. 1:16). The battle itself is described summarily as a series of battles that moved across the barren southland (v. 7). The Historian noted that Saul and the people spared the Amalekite king and the best of the spoil—precisely the things that should not have been kept according to the custom of the ban.

A new word (15:10-16).—While Saul was on his way back from the battle, Samuel received a new word that caused him anguish: Saul had disobeyed (v. 11)! Samuel's first reaction was anger, but it isn't clear whether his anger was directed toward Saul or God. His prayer to the Lord continued through the night (v. 11) and merged with an early morning departure to meet Saul. But Saul didn't appear; he had veered off to Gilgal in the Jordan Valley after setting up a victory monument celebrating his defeat of the Amalekites (v. 12). So Samuel went to Gilgal, the scene of the other painful meeting with Saul (13:8ff). Samuel cut the preliminary greetings short with a sharp question that implied condemnation (v. 14). Saul protested his innocence (v. 13) and immediately blamed the people for not carrying out Samuel's command: "They have brought them . . . " (v. 15).

The confrontation (15:17-33).—Samuel seems to have accepted Saul's contention that the people refused to destroy the spoils, but he condemned Saul for not exercising the leadership that was his by virtue of his office. In himself he was powerless, "little" (9:21), but as king he was the head of all the tribes and was responsible for commanding them. The pronouns in this section are painfully singular: "The Lord anointed *you*" (15:17); "Why then did *you* not obey?" (v. 19). It is in the light of this condemnation that Saul tried to distinguish between personal obedience and national disobedience: "*I* have obeyed . . . *I* have gone . . . *I* have brought . . . *I* have utterly destroyed" (v. 20). Perhaps Saul could have reminded Samuel that Joshua was not condemned for the sin of the people under his command who did a comparable thing (Josh. 7)! In Saul's case the "sin" was greater in magnitude but less reprehensible in motive; they violated the ban not for their own profit but ostensibly to perform their obedience "before men" back at camp (v. 21). Ultimately Saul's defense was a confession of his failure to lead his people; "I feared the people" (v. 24).

Samuel's condemnation of Saul stands out in 1 Samuel as a prophetic sermon. It resembles Hosea 6:6 where the prophet contrasted burnt offerings and sacrifices with steadfast love and knowledge of God. Samuel contrasted these religious rituals with obedience to the divine command which was paramount. Saul's sin was characterized as "rebellion" and "stubbornness" (v. 23) in the Revised Standard Version, but the *New English Bible* is more understandable: "Defiance of him is sinful as witchcraft, yielding to men as evil as idolatry." Thus a lack of obedience to the will of God is as wrong as actual perversions of religion.

The final scene of this tragic episode involves an accidental tearing away of Samuel's robe as Saul desperately grabbed for the departing prophet (v. 27). Samuel used the torn garment to pronounce the tearing away of Saul's kingdom (v. 28). But after Saul confessed his sin for the second time (vv. 24,30) Samuel agreed to appear with Saul before the elders. Apparently this endorsement was crucial to Saul. Samuel himself executed Agag "before the Lord," as a fulfillment of the original command (v. 33).

The final parting (15:34-35).—Samuel's departure marks a turning point in the story. The failure of Saul to have further contact with Samuel points to the rupture of that relationship. Later when Saul desperately needed a word from God there was no one left alive to mediate it. But the next verse notes that Samuel "grieved" for Saul, preparing the way for the opening scene of the following chapter.

David and Saul, Two Kings in the Land
16:1 to 31:13

David's Beginnings (16:1-23)

The anointing of David (16:1-13).—The breach between Samuel and Saul finally became irreparable (15:35), and this situation took its toll on Samuel as well as Saul. Samuel mourned over Saul (16:1). Once again, however, Samuel appears reluctant to release an institution that the Lord had decided to abandon: earlier it was a system of judgeship; now it was the dynasty of Saul. The word *rejected* echos through the Saul story like the slow drumbeat of a funeral procession. It prepares the way for the great promise that the Lord would never take his love from David (2 Sam. 7:15).

Samuel was sent to Bethlehem with a horn of oil (not a vial as in 10:1) to anoint one of the sons of Jesse. Bethlehem was a few miles south of Jerusalem and, thus, in Judah. The road from Ramah to Bethlehem would have passed through Saul's hometown of Gibeah. Only here among the accounts does Samuel ever seem threatened by Saul (v. 2), but Saul's later action against the priests of Nob indicates that Samuel had reason to fear (22:16ff). Samuel avoided suspicion by taking an animal to Bethlehem for a sacrifice. Years earlier he had conducted such a sacrifice for Saul's anointing. Bethlehem was not one of the cities Samuel regularly visited; thus his visit caused fear among the elders (v. 4), one of whom, presumably, was Jesse. Their question suggests that sometimes the prophet came not to pronounce peace but a sword (Amos 7:11). The fact that Samuel did not openly proclaim why he had come to Bethlehem may indicate that he feared Saul's reaction. But he had anointed Saul secretly, too, when there was no obvious threat to the prophet. Samuel consecrated the elders, including Jesse and his sons (v. 5). From this point on the elders play no role in the story; all eyes are directed to Jesse's sons. As earlier, when Samuel had successively narrowed the choice to Saul (10:21), so now he cast lots between the sons of Jesse. None of the first seven was chosen (v. 10). Eliab, Jesse's firstborn, had the physical attributes of Saul (10:23), but this time Samuel learned that physical appearance was not enough (v. 7, but see v. 12). The story stresses that both Samuel (v. 6) and Jesse (v. 10) assumed that one of the seven would be chosen. But the Lord's choice fell outside human expectations. The theme of the youngest being God's chosen (v. 11) is not new; both the Jacob-Esau cycle, the Joseph narratives, and the Moses story make the same point! The anointing took place "in the midst of his brothers" (v. 13), though apparently, not in full sight of the elders.

In many ways this account stands alone in the David story. While Bethlehem was important to later writers (Mic. 5:2), it played no role in the crowning of David as king (2 Sam. 2:1). In the Goliath episode (17:28) David certainly wasn't treated as an anointed one by his brothers. The main point was that the Lord had chosen David in advance, directed Samuel to him, and then confirmed his choice by the coming of his Spirit on David (16:13). Likewise the Spirit "departed" from Saul.

David's coming to Saul (16:14-23).—David's introduction to Saul, his entry into the royal court, was one of those coincidences so "right" that it struck the Historian as divinely guided. Young David had already been singled out by Samuel when Saul became ill (v. 14). To the Historian it was not unusual to say that an "evil spirit" could come "from the Lord." Indeed, at these early stages of the Israelite faith, people did not yet think in terms of a "Satan" as later generations would. To them the Lord guided history with supreme sovereignty. Thus he could be described as hardening Pharaoh's heart (Ex. 7:3) or sending a "lying spirit" to a prophet (1 Kings 22:22), or even attempting to kill Moses (Ex. 4:24). These theological descriptions are interpretations of historical events as due to the intervening hand of God. So in this case, to the Historian, Saul's depression became a sign of the rejection of God (16:14). To combat Saul's condition, his subordinates suggested music (v. 16), to which Saul agreed (v. 17). Someone suggested "a son of Jesse," and Saul then sent for the young man David (v. 19). Verse 18 makes it clear, however, that David was not just a musician; he was also known as a warrior, an able speaker, and a person of good appearance. The next chapter describes David as just such a warrior—but one who is unknown to Saul (17:58). Perhaps this seeming discrepancy can be attributed to the Historian's method of giving summary statements such as 16:21-22 and then telling a story that fills in the details.

Saul exercised one of the rights of the king mentioned by Samuel

(8:11) when he drafted David. David "entered his service" just as other "men of valor" (10:26) had done. That David became an armor-bearer for Saul (v. 21) may simply mean that David served in this capacity in Saul's army. Joab later had ten armor-bearers with him during a battle (2 Sam. 18:15), so the title does not imply a close personal relationship. However, David at some point did develop such a relationship through his musical ability (v. 23).

David and Goliath (17:1-58)

The challenge from Goliath (17:1-11).—Once again the Philistines challenged Israel. In this case the battleground lay in the low hills west of Bethlehem, David's home. The two armies camped on opposite sides of a valley (v. 3), and, following a Greek system of warfare, the Philistines challenged Israel to send out a single combatant (v. 8). Since the taunting procedure went on for a month (v. 16), it is clear that this was a border skirmish and not a battle for the purpose of conquest.

Goliath, a nine-foot giant according to the text (v. 4), appeared daily in his armor. Only Saul and Jonathan among the Israelites had armor (13:22). The armor consisted of a helmet, the chainlike coat of mail, and metal leg guards (greaves). Goliath also had metal weapons: a sword, a javelin (a small spear), and a heavy spear with a head weighing as much as a sixteen-pound sledgehammer.

Goliath's taunting (vv. 8-10) of Israel was indicative of the personal element in ancient warfare when armies stood within shouting distance of each other. Other examples include the Rabshakeh's speech before the walls of Jerusalem (Isa. 36:4-10) and Isaiah's reply (37:22), although these represent different situations. The effect of Goliath's size and his words was devastating (v. 11).

David's entry into the story (17:12-19).—The Historian wove together scenes from the battlefield (vv. 16,19), and the scene in Bethlehem as he brought David into the narrative. David was the youngest of eight (or seven, 1 Chron. 2:15) sons born to Jesse of Bethlehem. Jesse was too old to fight in the war but supported the war effort by sending supplies by David (v. 15). Each family sent provisions for its sons and additional supplies for the army in general (v. 18). Jesse sent David to his brothers with an ephah (about ten gallons) of roasted grain and ten loaves of bread. In addition he sent ten cheeses (literally, "slices of milk") for the entire unit of soldiers. What the brothers (or the officers?) might have sent back as proof of receipt (v. 18) is not known.

Saul's offer (17:20-30).—David's journey is passed over quickly, and the description resumes just as David reaches the Israelite camp. The soldiers were chanting a war cry as they went to the battlefield. David turned the food supplies over to the supply officer and joined the chanting troops in time to hear Goliath's taunt (vv. 10,23). The sentence, "David heard him" (v. 23) carries much more weight than these simple words normally would. The Historian was indicating that this hearing would make a difference. The words that struck terror in the hearts of strong men failed to awe the young David. He put the matter in its theological setting; no one should be able to defy the living God whom Israel served (v. 26), especially not an "uncircumcised Philistine." Thus, long before the apostle Paul's time, Hebrews knew themselves by the sign of their covenant with God. They were the circumcised (Eph. 2:11; Gal. 2:7).

When David heard tales of a great reward that would belong to the man who defeated Goliath, he reacted with dismay that such should be necessary. Goliath should be stopped because he defied Israel's God—not because his death could make a man a wealthy noble. But the rewards Saul offered (v. 25) play a significant role in the rest of the story. David was rewarded only by the women who sang of his fame (18:7); he was denied Saul's eldest daughter after being promised marriage to her (18:17); and his parents ultimately were driven from the land itself while David and his kinsmen were hunted as enemies of the state (22:1-4). In this way the Historian quietly began to note Saul's unjust treatment of David.

David's brothers responded to his remarks with sarcastic condescension (v. 28). There is no indication that this episode came *after* David had been anointed king in the presence of his brothers (16:13)! Once again the Historian's method of combining accounts raises questions for modern readers that he did not intend to raise.

David's response (17:31-40).—David's words reached Saul, who summoned him. David then officially offered to fight Goliath (v. 32). Saul first refused David, comparing his youth to Goliath's years of experience. (Apparently David was as big as other Israelite soldiers; his size was not an issue!) David's answer was that his experience in protecting a flock from lions and bears was ample experience. He was confident not in his own ability but in the continued help from the Lord (v. 37). Saul took a great risk in authorizing David to fight for Israel. Had David lost, the army would have lost its morale and fled before the Philistines. Thus Saul attempted to help David by providing his own armor—a treasure which only he and Jonathan had—and in so doing risked the loss of that which marked him as a king! But David felt restricted by the heavy protecting plates and chose instead a shepherd's weapons: slingshot, stones, and club.

A war of words (17:41-47).—This paragraph depicts the psychological side of ancient warfare. David and the Philistine called upon their God (or gods) and taunted each other. Each discounted the weapons of the other. The Historian has given David's speech much more space, since it expressed for him the great truth that the Lord was working in and through David. David viewed victory as a gift from the Lord who would "deliver" the Philistine into his hand (v. 46).

No sword in his hand (17:48-54).—The Philistine moved slowly; David ran quickly. The battle was over before the Philistine could throw his massive spear. Goliath fell on his face before the Lord's onslaught just as the Philistine idol, Dagon, had fallen before the ark (5:3). The fact that David conquered the giant with no sword in his hand was proof that the Lord had, indeed, delivered the enemy to David. David killed and decapitated Goliath with the Philistine's own sword, and the Philistines fled the battlefield. The single combat was the signal to begin the war, and Israel attacked with confidence, inspired by David's victory. After the enemy had been driven back to its own borders (v. 52), the Israelites took their equipment. Verse 54 seems to indicate what David did years later. Jerusalem did not belong to Israel until David conquered it (2 Sam. 5:6-10). The tent referred to may be the tent David prepared for the ark in Jerusalem (2 Sam. 6:17).

An introduction to Saul (17:55-58).—These verses assume that Saul did not know David and did not know who Goliath's opponent was! Thus, this episode is difficult to reconcile either with David's role as a musician for Saul (16:19-23) or with Saul's dialogue with David as he sent him forth to fight. It tells another version of how Saul came to know David and probably was once part of a slightly

different version of the Goliath narrative in which David slipped out
of camp to fight (like Jonathan earlier, chap. 14) and was not known
to Saul until after the battle.

Saul's Growing Jealousy (18:1-30)

David's fame grew rapidly. He was widely acclaimed even by
members of Saul's own family. But David's popularity quickly became a threat to Saul and suspicion grew like a dark cloud in the
mind of the king. Finally the dark cloud emptied itself in a series of
attempts on David's life. These verses show how Saul's suspicion and
jealousy drove him to plot secretly against the popular David.

David and Jonathan (18:1-5).—An immediate bond of friendship
developed between David and Saul's son, Jonathan. Following the
Philistine battle Saul kept David with him and did not let him return
to Jesse (v. 2). Jonathan "made a covenant" with David. Ultimately,
this covenant included an agreement that David would be king and
Jonathan would serve as the commander of the army (23:17). As a
symbol of the union between these two friends, Jonathan gave David
his princely robe and his armor. The heir to Saul's throne shared the
symbols of royalty with David. Even Saul recognized David's ability
and promoted him (v. 5).

David and Saul (18:6-16).—It is clear that the Historian does not
narrate events in a strictly chronological order. The episodes described here are best understood if that is kept in mind. David's victory over Goliath quickly became legendary, and it was sung about
by the women. Perhaps the song that is recorded celebrates more
than David's initial victory. It described David's victories as greater
than Saul's, and this popular praise of a subordinate aroused Saul's
suspicions. The statement, "What more can he have but the kingdom?" (v. 8) reflects a suspicion that David was plotting to overthrow Saul (see also 1 Kings 2:22).

The episode that follows (vv. 10-11) reflects the account of David
as a musician (16:14ff). In its present position it shows Saul's efforts
to rid himself of David under the guise of "a fit." Many interpret
these stories to reflect a state of depression or mental illness on Saul's
part. While this may be accurate, it is not necessarily so. Saul was
noted for his spirit-filled behavior (10:10-11; 19:23-24). The word

translated "rave" here (v. 10) is actually the word "prophesy." Prophecy could involve ecstatic dancing and agitated activity (1 Kings 18:26-29) as well as music (1 Sam. 10:5-6). Thus Saul apparently used such a moment as a cover for an attempt on David's life; the Historian described it as a deliberate act, not the unintended act of a sick soul! The Historian rightly described these acts as the result of an "evil spirit." Failing to kill David "accidentally," Saul sent him out to serve with the army, but this backfired, too, because "the Lord was with him" (v. 14).

David and Saul's daughters (18:16-30).—Saul had two daughters, Merab, the eldest, and Michal. He may have promised Merab to the person who defeated Goliath; people thought he had, at least (17:25). As if in fulfillment of that offer, Saul granted David Merab's hand in marriage following a suitable time of testing. The Historian interpreted this "testing" as an effort to let the Philistines get rid of David (18:17). When this plan failed, Saul refused to follow through with the marriage, giving Merab to another man (v. 19).

Essentially the same scene unfolds again when Michal falls in love with David (v. 20). The negotiations were carried on through intermediate sources with David protesting his inability to provide a suitable marriage present as a "poor man" (v. 23). Once again Saul requested only extensive success in battle against the Philistines: proof of the death of a hundred previously uncircumcised Philistines. A more gruesome marriage present could hardly be imagined, but David managed to offer twice the number of proven Philistine casualties. This time Saul gave his daughter in marriage, but he grew even more fearful of David. And well he might—for now David was legitimately part of the royal family, the king's son-in-law. A concluding note speaks of David's continued success against the Philistines and his increasing fame (v. 30).

David's Escape to Samuel (19:1-24)

It must be remembered that the Historian had to squeeze his long story into a small space. The reader should remember that time elapses without being noted. Saul's efforts to kill David apparently took place over a period of months if not years. In this chapter three major figures protect David from Saul: Jonathan, Michal, and

Samuel. The underlying idea is that Saul alone found reason to harm David; all others thought him innocent.

Jonathan intercedes for David (19:1-7).—For the first time Saul spoke openly of executing David as if David were a conspirator seeking to capture the throne. Jonathan informed David and interceded with Saul on David's behalf (v. 4). He characterized Saul's intended action not as a "police action" but as a "sin." David had not plotted against Saul; indeed, Jonathan reminded Saul that David once risked his life for him. To execute David would be to kill "without cause," (v. 5). Saul appeared to be convinced. He took an oath (v. 6) that David would not be executed, and Jonathan brought David back into the king's palace.

Renewed suspicion (19:8-10).—New successes in battle against the Philistines rekindled Saul's suspicions. Saul again hurled a spear at David as he provided music for Saul. This time David fled from the king's palace.

Michal saves David's life (19:11-17).—Although he fled from Saul, David seems not to have grasped even at this point that Saul was actually planning to execute him. Michal observed the men sent by Saul to watch his house and put two and two together (v. 11). To prevent the planned execution she lowered David out a (second story?) window to escape the guards. Then she used a "teraphim," a household god (Gen. 31:19) which was big enough to look like a human figure, to stall the first group Saul sent (v. 13). Her trick was discovered when Saul demanded that David be brought to him in bed if necessary. When her father accused Michal of helping David, she lied and blamed David for forcing her to help. The Historian did not condemn her. Instead he seemed to praise her wisdom and resourcefulness.

David flees to Samuel (19:18-24).—Once again the story does not quite fit with an earlier point. Samuel departed from Saul earlier and never saw him again (15:35), but here Saul prophesies before the aging prophet (v. 24). In addition, this is the second explanation given for the proverb, "Is Saul also among the prophets? . . . (10:11). Consequently, this episode is difficult to interpret.

David fled to Samuel for protection, explaining what Saul was doing. Samuel then went with David to Naioth, a place not yet located. Perhaps it was a section of the city of Ramah where a group of prophets lived. The messengers sent by Saul to get David were overcome by the Spirit of God. So instead of capturing David, three sets of messengers prophesied. Saul himself had the same experience, but entered more fully into the prophetic activity. For nakedness associated with prophets see Isaiah 20:3 and Micah 1:8, where it is a sign of deep mourning.

While the events mentioned here cannot be illuminated much, the Historian's purpose is clear. The Lord himself shielded David by his Spirit.

Jonathan's Effort to Save David (20:1-42)

The Historian wrote with one eye fixed on the future as he prepared this account. The story not only explains how David was warned to flee; it establishes Jonathan's innocence beyond question and prepares for David's later faithfulness to Jonathan's son, Mephibosheth (2 Sam. 9). It probes more deeply still into the reason for Saul's actions, stressing Saul's distress that his son will be displaced by David. Saul believed that David was planning a revolution.

Jonathan's innocence (20:1-11).—Either the reader must assume a lapse of time between this chapter and the preceding one (see 19:1 and 20:2) or understand these two episodes to be independent of each other. Here Jonathan is apparently ignorant of Saul's intention to execute David. Since he believed that his father consulted him on every issue, he felt justified in saying that David was mistaken: "It is not so" (v. 2). But David convinced Jonathan to test his understanding by noting Saul's reaction when David failed to appear at dinner on two consecutive evenings (v. 5). Jonathan was to offer a plausible excuse for David (v. 6) which would be accepted unless Saul planned to arrest David. An outburst of anger would betray his frustration at being foiled again (v. 7). David urged Jonathan himself to kill him if there was any fault in him. This again brought an affirmation of David's innocence from Jonathan (v. 9). They went to the field where David would hide to plan the signals to be used.

David's oath to Jonathan (20:12-17).—This section is difficult to place in the sequence of events. In the preceding unit David and Jonathan moved outside, and in the next unit they are in the field planning their signals. Here nothing is said about signals. Instead Jonathan will determine Saul's attitude and "send" (a messenger?) to

tell David (v. 12). But more puzzling still is the fact that even though
David is in danger, Jonathan speaks as if his own life is more immediately threatened (v. 14). Jonathan had covenanted with David to
yield the throne to him. He asked David's oath that when that happened David would not do as new kings usually did and kill all of the
remaining royal family (v. 15). This David swore (v. 17), and, later,
he kept his word to the surviving son of Jonathan (2 Sam. 9).

   The signals (20:18-23).—The new moon (v. 18) was the time
when the king expected his officials to gather for dinner. This meal
fell on the next day, and by the day after that David's absence would
require explanation (v. 19). Jonathan directed David to hide where
he had hidden previously. The phrase "when the matter was in
hand" (v. 19) is not a clear reference to anything now in the text.
The place is likewise vague, though it seems to have been a well-
known rock formation. Jonathan's signal consisted of his words to
the boy who retrieved his arrows. If he told the boy to go on further
to find the arrows, David was to "go further" away (v. 22). The
opposite remark would indicate that David could safely return.
They parted after Jonathan's reminder of their mutual vows about
their future relations (v. 23).

   Saul's reaction (20:24-34).—The scene opens in the king's palace
at the dinner hour. Abner, Saul's army commander, sat next to Saul,
and Jonathan sat at the other end of the table. There probably
would have been several others at the table, too, but David's place
was conspicuously absent. (It would be an interesting bit of trivia to
know what types of food were served and how, but that can't be
determined now.) Saul questioned David's absence on the second
evening, as Jonathan knew he would. The tension in the room must
have been high as the guests sat down to eat. One indication of this
was Saul's use of David's family name rather than his familiar name
(v. 27), which Jonathan used. Jonathan gave the excuse that David
had previously arranged (v. 6). It is interesting that David's brother
(Eliab?) acted as the head of the family though Jesse was still alive
(22:3-5).

   Saul immediately saw through the deception and cursed his own
son (v. 30) with language comparable to today's gutter language. He
accused Jonathan of choosing David (and again he avoided the name
itself) "to your own shame" (v. 30). Saul's charge was that Jonathan's
agreement with David was a shameful abdication that also brought

disgrace on his father. "To the shame of your mother's nakedness" may have meant that Jonathan's action had caused the father as much shame as would the public display of his wife's nakedness. It may also imply that Jonathan's action had disgraced the act of conceiving him, casting shame on his father's otherwise noble and honorable act (see Jer. 20:14-18). For Saul the continuation of his dynasty in Jonathan's reign was of paramount importance. Had he only known that such was not to be, how differently might his life have been lived? But such opportunity to shape life by its outcome is not given to anyone! The importance of this issue generated such high passion in Saul that he acted completely irrationally, hurling his spear at the son he wanted so much to succeed him as king (v. 33)! Though he missed, his words had hit home, and the son he loved left the table infuriated, humiliated, and hurt because of his father's treatment of David (v. 34). These two noble men saw two completely different sides of David.

The final departure of David (20:35-42).—The scene in the field requires little comment except to note that the elaborate signal seems to have been unnecessary because Jonathan spoke to David personally (v. 41ff). The key element is the repetition once again of the covenant relationship between the two. Ultimately when Jonathan was dead no one could testify that Jonathan had wanted David to be king. The Historian emphasized this part of David's past to establish David's right to rule later and also to interpret David's treatment of Jonathan's son.

Saul's Vengeance on the Priests of Nob (21:1 to 22:23)

High drama and sickening tragedy blend in these verses that mark a turning point in the Saul/David story. From this point on David no longer acts or suffers alone. David's flight became open treason in the eyes of Saul, and he treated it as such. Ultimately, David himself began to treat his "war" with Saul as a quest for the kingship, and he began to prepare to become the next king. In all of this fever of activity the Historian perceived the hand of God moving, though he does not blame God for the tragic errors in judgment on the part of these two men.

David's flight to Nob (21:1-9).—David fled south toward Bethlehem. David's first stop was at the priestly city of Nob. This town was so close to Jerusalem that an attacking army could camp there and "shake his fist" at the capital city (Isa. 10:32). Ahimelech, the priest in charge of Nob, met David. The fact that he was trembling (v. 1) indicates that he sensed danger in this (midnight?) meeting. David was alone, unarmed, and without provisions but several miles from Gibeah, the capital. Certainly this was unusual. David lied to Ahimelech, as Michal and Jonathan lied to Saul (v. 2), explaining his lack of provisions as the result of a mission that required secrecy. The priest offered "the bread of the Presence" to David and his men, who would supposedly join in, if they were ritually clean (see Ex. 19:15). Perhaps David's assertions that "of a truth, women have been kept from us" was a tongue in cheek observation, for he himself had been driven from his wife!

Having gotten food, David asked about weapons and learned that Goliath's sword was there. Ahimelech offered it without question to David noting that it was behind the "ephod" (v. 9). The ephod here seems to be some type of furniture rather than part of a robe.

Tucked in the middle of this episode (v. 7) there is just a glimpse of a sinister figure. Doeg the Edomite who was part of Saul's staff saw and heard this conversation. The Historian warns us that David's flight was no longer a secret; surely Doeg will reappear later (22:9).

David's first flight to the Philistines (21:10-15).—David went to Achish, king of Gath, twice, according to the Historian (see also chap. 27). The first attempt to find refuge with the very enemy he had fought so successfully was rebuffed. The entire account may belong elsewhere, for it is not likely that David strode into a Philistine camp carrying the sword of Goliath! If indeed David twice went to Gath it shows his determination to join the neighboring Philistines rather than flee a great distance. Apparently his goal was not to abandon Israel but to remain in close contact with it. Otherwise he would have fled to Moab (22:3ff) where he would have been safe but removed from Israel.

This account is made up of a speech by the servants of Achish, a report of David's behavior, and a speech by Achish. The servants recognized David as "king," which reflects his later status, and as a great warrior—but not as the slayer of Goliath, which is strange. But since he was known to them, David's plan was destroyed, and he then had to escape both from Achish and Saul! He escaped from the Philistines by playing insane, thereby convincing Achish that he was not David. The Historian has, however, managed to make Achish a prophet of things to come by having him ask "Shall this fellow come into my house?" (v. 15), which, of course, David did later!

The beginning of David's "revolt" (22:1-5).—Up to this point David had acted as an individual, and there was no hint other than Saul's suspicions that he was actively trying to overthrow the king. When David gathered a small army of kinsmen from Judah and others who were dissatisfied with Saul's reign (v. 2), he was in open rebellion against the king. David's army of four hundred was smaller than Saul's (26:2) but almost the size of the army that faced the Philistines earlier (13:15). The Historian specifically noted that David's army contained people in debt and others who were oppressed. The institution of kingship had apparently already caused social upheaval in Israel!

The fact that David took his immediate family out of the country is another indication that the conflict had moved beyond the stage of personal conflict. The land of Moab was on the other side of the Dead Sea from Judah. According to the book of Ruth, David's ancestors were Moabites.

The sudden introduction of Gad, a prophet or seer (2 Sam. 24:11), is unlike the Historian, who usually prepares his readers for each new character (as he did with Doeg, for example). Nothing is known of this prophet. He warned David to flee from his hiding place and move into open country, perhaps to avoid getting trapped. The Historian thus points to the intervention of God that preserved David from Saul.

Doeg's report to Saul (22:6-10).—Saul soon discovered where David was and that he had gathered an army. He berated his own "servants," in this case government and army officials, accusing them of helping David. Saul's remark about "fields and vineyards" (v. 7) opens a window on the way kings ruled then. The king granted land to his officials as a form of pay. He was either questioning whether David could treat them as he had done and thus woo them away, or reminding those present that they owed their lands and positions not to David but to him. Saul went so far as to accuse his servants of "conspiring" against him—an act punishable by death in any kingdom! He accused Jonathan of inciting David, and all of them of withholding information (v. 8). Then Doeg confessed that he had seen David with Ahimelech. Like Saul, Doeg referred to David as "the son of Jesse" (vv. 7,9), choosing not to use the familiar name. Doeg added that he had seen Ahimelech "inquire" for David; in this context the implication was that Ahimelech had helped David decide whether to rebel by asking the Lord's will. No reference to this appeared in the earlier account.

Saul's execution of the priests of Nob (22:11-19).—Saul brought Ahimelech and all the other priests of Nob, descendants of Eli, the priest at Shiloh, to Gibeah for a trial. He repeated the charges made by Doeg (v. 13). Ahimelech responded by noting David's place of honor in Saul's administration and in his family, protesting that he had sought divine guidance for David many times. He argued that his actions were normal rather than subversive. But Saul's mind was made up; he sentenced all the priests to death and immediately ordered his guards to execute them because they did not tell him that David had fled (v. 16). But the soldiers refused to execute the priests! Their revulsion at Saul's order was apparent, and doubtless many others shared their feelings. Certainly the Historian did. Doeg, the Edomite, who had not confessed until placed in a dangerous situation himself, carried out the gruesome command. Eighty-five priests fell; obviously the guard must have assisted. But the slaughter did not end there. The city itself was treated as an enemy city, and every living thing was slaughtered. It is hard to comprehend the butchery this involved. It was intended, perhaps, as a warning to others and seems to have succeeded (see the next chapter). But it is difficult to understand why no divine rejection was reported here. Perhaps the Historian viewed it as the act of a man already alienated from the Lord.

Abiathar becomes David's priest (22:20-23).—Abiathar somehow escaped the massacre and fled to David carrying the sad news from Nob. David expressed grief at having caused the death of a city but welcomed Abiathar. From this point on Abiathar was a most significant person. He was the last surviving descendant of Eli, and he was on David's side. Saul had none of this line of priests to "inquire" for him, though he may have had others. Thus in a real sense David had access to God that Saul denied himself, a fact that Saul would feel very keenly later.

David in Flight from Saul (23:1-29)

The full effects of Saul's action against Nob become clear in this chapter. Even a city that David rescued from Philistine marauders was afraid to befriend David because they feared the greater power of Saul. When David fled to the wilderness area which was south of his own hometown, the people reported his presence to Saul (vv. 19-20). But at the same time, Abiathar was able to give the Word of God to David and advise him properly (vv. 6-12).

David saves Keilah (23:1-6).—The Philistines moved into the low hills separating them from Judah and took the harvested grain from the threshing floors—the flat spots where the grain was separated from the straw and chaff (see also Judg. 6:3-6,11). In a time when each city depended entirely on the grain it grew for its food (there was little grain for market in the ancient world) such a raid could well spell famine and death—or at the least a forced departure to other places that had grain. (See Gen. 42; the closest grain was in Egypt.) The city of Keilah (pronounced Kuh-ee-lah) was in desperate trouble, and the central government headed by Saul had not responded. To decide whether to help, David "inquired" of the Lord; that is, he consulted the ephod containing the sacred lots, Urim and Thummim (v. 6). Such a procedure produced only a yes or no answer, so David phrased questions that could be answered that way. The divine answer was "Go," but David's men hesitated (v. 3). A second inquiry confirmed the first, and David defeated the Philistines. The word *delivered* is the same as the word "saved."

Keilah would betray David (23:6-14).—The Historian pointed to the significance of Abiathar's presence with David. He had managed to bring the ephod, the garment or box used to consult the sacred lots. It would be needed to help David escape. The Historian described David's dilemma by telling what Saul "thought"—David had reentered an enclosed city where he could be captured (see 22:5). If the city was willing to resist Saul, David would be safe inside; but if the city opened its gates to Saul, David would be destroyed.

Although David and his soldiers had saved Keilah from the Philistine marauders, the consultation of the lots indicated that they would turn David over to Saul (23:7). Apparently even David's army—now six hundred strong—was not enough margin of safety for the people of the city. So David and his group left the city. He

moved eastward to the wilderness area southeast of Hebron called
the Wilderness of Ziph (pronounced Zeeph). The Historian noted
that success in military matters depended on God's "gift," and God
did not "give" David into Saul's hand!

Jonathan's covenant with David (23:15-18).—Saul actively pursued David, and David's situation was grave (v. 15). While David
moved about in the open country southeast of Hebron, Jonathan
came to him. The Historian did not tell how Jonathan knew his location or what risks he took in coming. The report is skimpy, reempha-
sizing once again that Jonathan had covenanted to make David king
and himself army commander ("next to you"). Such a symbolic visit
would have "strengthened" David's hand greatly but, surely, it went
unknown among Saul's people!

The populace betrays David (23:19-29).—Once again, possibly
because they feared the consequences of sheltering David, the people
in the southern wilderness reported David's presence to Saul. But
information flowed both ways; David was told (v. 25). Perhaps
Jonathan played a part in helping David with such information,
though this is never said. Saul asked his informers for precise information and again entered the field against David (v. 25). David had
moved further south to the area of Maon, a few miles from Ziph and
Horesh. The "Arabah" usually means the barren depression extending from the Dead Sea to the Gulf of Aqabah, but here it seems to
include the dry highlands south of Hebron (v. 24). The pursuers
were within one mountain ridge of David's men when a messenger
arrived to call Saul to battle with the Philistines (v. 27). One almost
expects the Historian to add—"and God did not give David into
Saul's hand again!"

The Sparing of Saul at Engedi (24:1-22)

When Saul resumed the chase, David had moved to Engedi, a
lush, tropical area near the western shore of the Dead Sea. Here, in a
large cave, David had the opportunity to kill Saul but would not.
The Historian has kept two stories like this (see also chap. 26). They
show David's innocence in a convincing manner, so convincing that
even Saul acknowledged it openly.

The scene in the cave (24:1-7).—Saul took a large expedition into the rugged hills west of the Dead Sea (v. 2). The name of the area, "Wildgoats' Rocks" indicates that the terrain was not flat! The hills in this area have numerous caves. The scene in the cave is hard to reconstruct. It involves one of life's elemental necessities, having a bowel movement. The darkness of the cave Saul chose to use happened to shelter David and his men. How David could have cut off some of Saul's clothing without being detected is not discussed either. All attention was focused on the fact that because Saul was the Lord's anointed (v. 6) David resisted the urging of his men to kill the king (v. 4). He even felt guilty for cutting his robe (v. 4)!

The presentation of the evidence (24:8-15).—After Saul left the cave David showed himself—presumably at a safe distance—and did obeisance (v. 9). Once again the Historian has stressed the complete uprightness of David; he paid the proper respect to the king whom he refused to harm. David presented the piece of Saul's robe (v. 11) and demonstrated that he could have killed Saul. His refusal to do so was proof that "there is no wrong or treason" intended in his actions. David's protest continued in the form of a prayer for vengeance upon Saul, but he affirmed that he himself would not exact the vengeance (compare Jer. 11:20). Wickedness comes from wicked people according to the proverb David used, but not from him (v. 13). The king has spent his time chasing someone as harmless as a flea! Thus David invoked the Lord's judgment between them. The language is the language of the courtroom. He asked the Lord to notice his case ("see to it," v. 15), argue for him, pass down a sentence of innocent and, thus, deliver him from his enemy.

Saul's response (24:16-22).—Saul's words do not fit with his subsequent actions. Here he seemed to surrender his case against David completely and even acknowledged that David would be king after him (v. 20). He obviously changed his mind later and resumed the chase. Perhaps Saul's behavior *was* subject to great shifts; if so, the Historian clearly emphasized Saul's inconsistent stances. In the larger context of the entire story this episode demonstrates that Saul himself confessed David's righteousness (v. 17), blessed David (v. 19), and asked mercy from David upon his descendants (v. 21). Though this text says that David swore not to "cut off" Saul's descendants, David did precisely that after he became king. The gruesome story of this event is recounted in 2 Samuel 21.

David and Abigail (25:1-44)

The death of Samuel (25:1a).—This detached note prepares the way for a tragic episode later when Saul needed Samuel (28:3ff). One can imagine the elaborate funeral that an important figure such as Samuel would have received. The people buried Samuel in his house—apparently not an uncommon form of burial (1 Kings 2:34).

David's request to Nabal (25:1b-8).—From the region near the Dead Sea David took his band of warriors further south. The wilderness of Paran is far to the south in the Sinai peninsula. However, the other places mentioned, Maon and Carmel, are not far south of Ziph and Keilah mentioned earlier (23:1,24). Thus the locale is central Judah. A man lived there with a name that closely matched his behavior—Nabal (fool). Nabal was a wealthy herder, with a wife who could have been the model for Proverbs 31:10ff. Abigail contrasts sharply with her husband. She was wise and gentle; Nabal was foolish and ill-natured (v. 3). The fact that he was a Calebite may have been meant to stress either his animal nature (Caleb means "dog" in Hebrew!) or his membership in the honored clan that controlled the major city of Hebron (Judg. 1:20). Perhaps the name was meant to sound both notes.

David sent ten warriors to receive a gift from Nabal for protecting his flocks! While this sounds closely akin to extortion to modern ears, there is no note of condemnation in the text. David is pictured as requesting sustenance while reminding Nabal that his army of six hundred men had not lived off his flocks while they roamed the hills. The young man's greeting stressed the note of peace three times over (25:6). The time of shearing was a time of celebrating and feasting among the herders.

Nabal's response (25:9-13).—The young men carried David's message and repeated it verbatim for Nabal. The oral messenger's speech did then what a letter would do now. The fact that Nabal kept them waiting indicates that his answer was premeditated. When it came it was couched in the language of ridicule (David who?) and insult (v. 11). Nabal knew very well who David was, but he chose to treat him with contempt, as if he were a runaway slave instead of a political refugee. The young messengers repeated Nabal's words to David. David's response was limited to the terse order to prepare for battle. It is perhaps instructive to note here, also, that the Historian always describes action through direct speech rather than through description. David's few words convey both action and atmosphere.

Abigail receives the news (25:14-17).—Nabal's young men informed Abigail of their master's abusive language ("he railed at them") and testified to the protection received from David's men. David's troops were a "wall" to them (Ex. 14:22), protecting them (25:16). They urged Abigail to act wisely ("know" and "consider") to divert the attack which was sure to come. Nabal was too abusive to be approached (v. 17).

Abigail's journey (25:18-22).—The food stuff Abigail assembled included bread, wine, dressed sheep, grain, raisins, and figs. The quantities are proportionate to the six-hundred-man size of David's army. One wonders how much time would have been required to prepare such quantities of bread! Abigail sent the food ahead of her as Jacob had done earlier when he met a supposedly angry Esau (Gen. 32:13ff). Abigail followed.

At this point the Historian switched to the scene in David's group. David's anger and his intention to destroy Nabal's house are portrayed as if David were talking to himself (vv. 21-22). The oath formula, "God do so," implies some drastic penalty if the oath taker fails to keep his vow.

Abigail's encounter with David (25:23-31).—Upon meeting David's company Abigail promptly prostrated herself in submission to David. Before David ever got a word in, this beautiful and charming woman had won her case! Her long speech (vv. 24-31) sought to dismiss Nabal's words as the babbling of a fool from whom one could expect nothing sensible and to place the blame on her own negligence (v. 24). Her trespass (v. 25) consisted in not seeing his messengers when they came—as if this were her responsibility which she had neglected! But Abigail demonstrated her wisdom in her evaluation of the consequences of David's planned action. Abigail argued that by accepting her present and foregoing the attack on Nabal, David would help himself when he became "prince" over Israel. According to her analysis David would become prince because his battles with Saul were "the battles of the Lord" (v. 28) and

the Lord was protecting his life (v. 29). Moreover, Abigail spoke as if
she knew of the prophecy of Nathan, still years in the future, when
she noted that the Lord would make David "a sure house" (2 Sam.
7:16) and would do all he had promised David (25:30). When David
became king, Abigail argued, he surely would not want to be known
as a man of blood (v. 31), and if he took vengeance as he planned, he
would go far beyond what the Lord allowed and be guilty of murder. It is interesting to note that precisely this charge of blood guilt
was eventually hurled at David by descendants of Saul (2 Sam.
16:7). Abigail ended her speech with a plea for her own safety (v.
31). Abigail's speech marks her as a wise woman who could see the
meaning of events better than either Nabal or David, both of whom
acted rashly and unwisely. It also makes the point that even though
David ended up with Nabal's wife, and presumably his property,
he did not incur blood guilt in the process.

David's reaction (25:32-35).—David's threefold blessing combines
a standard greeting formula with an acknowledgement that the
Lord had sent Abigail and her wisdom to him. David sent her away
in peace after receiving her gifts (v. 35).

The death of Nabal (25:36-38).—When Abigail returned it was
evening. The festival celebrating the sheep shearing was in full swing
(v. 36), and Nabal was "very drunk." Had David's army struck that
night there would have been little resistance! When Nabal was
sober Abigail told him how close disaster had approached, and the
news apparently brought on a stroke or some similar attack (compare 4:18). Nabal died within days of the episode. The Historian
judged that Nabal's death was an act of God (v. 38).

David marries Abigail (25:39-42).—In David's mind, the death of
Nabal represented the just punishment for Nabal's humiliating
insult. David's attitude here is a far cry from that of Jesus and can't
serve as a model for Christians. But surely this episode affords a
firsthand glimpse of the attitude toward enemies which formed the
background for Jesus' teaching on forgiveness (Matt. 5:44).

Note also that there was no thought here of a law of levirate marriage (Deut. 25:5-10) such as that assumed in Ruth (3:12ff). Abigail
was free to marry whomever she chose. David wooed her through
third parties—as was proper (see Gen. 24:4). Abigail's response (v.
41) was couched in the formal language of the ancient Semitic

world—suitable then but hardly acceptable for use in modern marriage rituals.

David's wives (25:43-44).—The Historian noted without elaboration another of David's marriages. Ahinoam of Jezreel—in the same area as Carmel—was the mother of a second son, Chileab, of whom little is known. Michal, David's first wife, was given to another man when David fled.

The Sparing of Saul at Hachilah (26:1-25)

This chapter is in many ways a duplicate of chapter 24, although details differ. This chapter is more readily understandable; slipping into and out of a camp undetected poses fewer problems than the scene in the cave. Moreover, Saul's words here are more in character. He does not admit that David would be king nor does he plead for mercy to his descendants. But both stories serve the same general purpose of proving David's blameless behavior toward Saul.

Saul returns to the chase (26:1-5).—Once again the inhabitants of Ziph in southeastern Judah informed Saul of David's whereabouts. Their action probably reflected less hostility to David than fear of reprisal from Saul. The incident at Nob (chaps. 21-22) evidently struck fear in the heart of the populace. When Saul's force encamped off the road, David sent a group of scouts ("spies," v. 4) to determine exactly where he was. Then David led a group of men to the encampment of Saul by night. Saul's camp seems to have been in open country with little to prevent David from observing it from a high point. He could even pick out the king lying in the midst of his army with Abner, his commander nearby.

David's entry into Saul's camp (26:6-12).—David asked two of his elite soldiers for a volunteer to go with him. The mission was obviously highly dangerous. Ahimelech the Hittite was a foreigner, and nothing more is known of him. Abishai, however, was the brother of Joab, who became David's commander later. Abishai ranked very high among David's officers (2 Sam. 23:18-19). Abishai volunteered to go with David into the midst of the enemy camp that slept so soundly that the Historian said they had been divinely anesthetized (v. 12). The "deep sleep" mentioned here translates the same word

used for Adam's sleep (Gen. 2:21). Once again David's soldier interpreted Saul's vulnerability as an indication that God had "given"
him to David. Abishai wanted to kill Saul with his own spear—the
spear that had been hurled at David—but again David refused.
David mused philosophically that Saul would die by a sudden stroke
from God (like Nabal, 25:38), or reach his time to die naturally, or
be killed in battle (v. 10). As before, David expected the Lord to
avenge the wrongs done him. This is a far different picture of David
than that sketched in the last chapter, where only a wise woman prevented David from a massacre comparable to that of Nob. Perhaps
the Historian intended to contrast David's behavior to a normal
enemy like Nabal and "the Lord's anointed." The repeated emphasis on David's absolute innocence in his dealings with Saul may have
been needed to balance later public opinion that David was "a man
of blood" himself. So instead of using the spear on Saul, they took the
spear and the water jug and left with evidence that they could have
killed Saul!

Presenting the evidence (26:13-16).—After putting a valley
between them, David called to Abner with a taunt and a rebuke.
Like the disciples in Gethsemane, Abner was unable to "keep watch"
through the night. He had failed to protect the king. The spear and
the water jug were proof of that (v. 16)! Abner plays a key role later
as the commander of Israel who turned over his soldiers to David
after a long, bitter fight. He was then murdered by Joab (2 Sam.
3:27). Although Abner has been mentioned repeatedly (14:50,51;
17:55,57; 20:25), he has never been an important part of any scene.
But he will be!

David's dialogue with Saul (26:17-25).—This long-distance conversation resembles the earlier one (chap. 24). David stressed his
innocence and his insignificance (vv. 18,20), and implied that Saul's
rage must have been inspired by men who should be cursed for the
injustice done to David. David apparently thought there was a con-
spiracy against *him* among Saul's advisers ("they have driven me
out," v. 19). David's plea "let not my blood fall to the earth away
from the presence of the Lord" (v. 20) can be interpreted several
ways. It may be a prayer that he would not die abroad. It may be a
protest against being "driven out," a plea that he be allowed to
return. It may be a prayer that he be allowed to die in the Lord's
land so the Lord would take vengeance for him. This assumes the

belief that the Lord's power and involvement was limited to the national territory. Of these the first seems more likely in the context.

Saul's response here was limited to a general admission of wrongdoing (v. 21) and a general blessing on David (v. 25). David returned Saul's spear with a prayer that it would be done unto him as he had done it to others (v. 24)!

David Flees to the Philistines (27:1-12)

When a prominent military figure defects to the enemy there would be no possibility of that person regaining power in his native land. But David did precisely that. One reason he was able to do so was his ability to explain his defection as a forced flight. Another was his ability to maintain close ties with Judah even while living in Philistine territory. Questions abound! Why did he not flee to Moab? Why did he flee west to the hated Philistines? What was David's religious life like in Philistia? What were his relationships with the native inhabitants? How did he arrange to join the Philistines? These questions were never addressed by the Historian. This fact emphasizes once again that the reader must be willing to see what the Historian chose to describe!

The transition to Gath (27:1-4).—David's inner thoughts must have been debated at length by his leaders before such a change was made. Perhaps David chose to go to Philistia rather than Moab because Saul would think him politically dead and stop the war (v. 1). A transition to a neutral country may have continued the chase. For the first time the Historian noted the presence of "families" with David's six hundred men (v. 2). This would have swelled their numbers considerably. David's wives received special mention here and will be referred to again later. David's strategy worked; Saul gave up—or considered the victory won (v. 4).

David receives a city (27:5-7).—These verses should perhaps be read after the next paragraph (vv. 8-12). David's request to Achish (pronounced Ah-keesh) assumes that he had served Achish for a long period and was requesting a favor if Achish had found him trustworthy. Achish granted David a city, Ziklag, that lay on the border between Philistia and Judah. The Historian noted that this city remained David's after he left the Philistines and still belonged to

Judah in his own day. David's time in Philistia—presumably the
time in Gath and Ziklag—was sixteen months.

The explanation for David's acceptance (27:8-12).—David
became in effect a double agent! He sent his men on the marauding
raids other Philistines had practiced (23:1), but he attacked only
enemies of the Judeans. The Girzites are unknown. Amalekites were
the ancient enemy of Israel (see chap. 15). The Geshurites mentioned here lived between Philistia and Egypt, to the south (see Josh.
13:2-3). But while he attacked Israel's enemies, he reported to
Achish that he was plundering Judah, the southern part of the
Hebrew lands (v. 10), and David saw to it that none whom he attacked lived to set the record straight (vv. 9,11). David's tactic was
as effective then as it is ungodly and repulsive now. It convinced
Achish that David could never go back (v. 12). Later the Historian
notes that David used the loot that he gathered to send gifts to the
cities of Judah and reminded them that he was not their enemy
(30:26-31).

The Beginning of the End (28:1-25)

The great drama that had been building nears its finale here. Saul
had driven away the one who had previously kept the Philistines at
bay and now had to face them alone. He had butchered the priests of
Nob who could have sought God's Word for him. Now he had to
cry out to God for himself without hearing a divine response. He had
outlived the prophet who called him and sent him to battle against
these Philistines and carried a burdened memory of their painful
parting. Now he had to start the battle alone without the powerful
stimulus the great prophet could have provided. It was a time when
the collected debts of the past were being called in—and Saul had no
reserves.

David's plight (28:1-2).—Achish of Gath granted David a city but
required a lifetime commitment of military service in battle as a
price (v. 2). The Philistines prepared to fight Israel, and there was no
way David could avoid fighting against his own people. To do so
would clearly have cut him off from any return.

Saul's plight (28:3-7).—Saul's troubles were spiritual as well as
physical. The Historian provided a background note (v. 3) to explain

why Saul's forthcoming action was so serious. The king himself had forbidden people to seek divine guidance by consulting the native "mediums and wizards." These were alternatives to the accepted means of inquiring of the Lord (dreams, sacred lots, and prophetic oracles, v. 6). In addition to this action which restricted access to God outside the official channels, Samuel, through whom the prophetic word had come (3:21), was dead—and the priests had been annihilated. While the latter was left unstated, it surely was understood as a factor here.

The Philistines gathered in the broad valley of Jezreel while the Hebrews assembled high on the hill of Gilboa which bordered the valley (v. 4). The Philistines dominated the level territory. Saul looked down on the gathering Philistines and "was afraid" and "trembled" (see the comment on 21:1). Saul desperately needed a word from God, much like a later king who sought such a word from the prophet he had imprisoned (Jer. 37:17). But God did not answer Saul (v. 6). "Dreams" were either revelations received by individuals while they slept at sacred spots (Gen. 28:12ff) or dreams received by prophets (Jer. 23:28). "Urim" refers to the sacred lot which the priest manipulated to determine God's will (Ex. 28:30), while "prophets" were those persons who heard God's message apart from the priestly ritual and acted as God's messengers. None of these means had given Saul a word from God. In desperation he turned to the very practice he himself had made illegal (28:7)—and his servants knew immediately where this illegal activity could be secured! He sought out a woman who was "a lady of ghosts," a person supposed to be able to commune with the dead.

Bringing up Samuel (28:8-14).—The village of Endor was several miles away and across the valley where the Philistines gathered. He made the trip at night (v. 8). Saul delayed telling the woman the person with whom he wished to speak because it would reveal his own identity (v. 12). Only Saul still needed to speak to Samuel! At first the woman refused because this kind of activity was illegal, and she did not know the people. It could have been a trap (v. 9). Saul's oath was surety enough for her to proceed (v. 10), and after she guessed who he was, he reassured her of immunity from punishment (v. 13). The dialogue that follows indicates that only the woman "saw" anything. She described for Saul the figure of the aged Samuel, but skeptics would say that the description would fit any elderly man (v. 14)! The woman called Samuel a "god" (v. 13). The word *elohim* may mean a deity or deities or simply a divine figure as opposed to a human figure. The latter seems to be meant here. Hebrews believed that every person entered a watery place beneath the earth called Sheol. It was neither a place of punishment nor reward but a place where the person was at rest (Job 14:12-13). Thus the woman described Samuel as "coming up out of the earth" (28:13). The woman's suggestion was enough to let Saul "know" that it was Samuel.

Saul's conversation with Samuel (28:15-19).—Questions abound at this point! Did Saul actually commune with the dead Samuel? Did he alone hear? How did others know what transpired? The Historian gave an answer to none of these questions. It is clear, however, that he believed the dialogue to convey divine truth to all. Saul heard again the words of rejection spoken years earlier by the living Samuel (v. 17). It was as if the rich man had been told that a voice from the dead would not sway a person who failed to obey the available truth (Luke 16:30-31). Saul's rejection for his failure to carry out the ban against Amalek (chap. 15) remained in force. The Lord had become Saul's "enemy" (v. 16) and had "torn the kingdom" from his hand and given it to David who is now named specifically (v. 17; 15:28). Coupled with this fresh reminder of his rejection, Saul heard the announcement of doom upon him, his family, and his nation (v. 19). It was a bitter word from God!

This conversation serves to interpret the meaning of a crushing defeat that brought Israel to its knees. The Lord was tearing the kingdom from Saul and transferring it to David. The agony and loss that must have sent a shudder through Israel were part of the work of God (Isa. 28:21).

Saul's reaction (28:20-25).—Saul collapsed from physical weakness and sheer terror (v. 20). The woman who had mediated the terrifying message ministered to Saul's physical needs, helping to restore his strength. Like Sarah of an earlier age (Gen. 18:6ff), the woman shared what she had with the king and his servants. The scene closes with a note that they went on their way. It ought to be remembered that this king walked all night to be with his army for the battle. He could have fled, but didn't.

"And Saul went to meet his end, a great soul face to face with a ravelled world, who refuses to turn his back on what he has taken upon him, but also a great soul with a fatal defect in his nature, not quite big enough to do the thing which his time demanded from its leader, but doing all which it was left possible for him to do."[1]

David's Release from Battle (29:1-11)

The setting for this crucial scene is the city of Aphek on the coastal plain north of Gath. It was the site of the earlier battle in which the Philistines captured the ark (4:1). The episode consists of two scenes. The first scene describes the conversation between Achish, king of Gath, and the other commanders (29:2-5). The second scene reports a later conversation between Achish and David (vv. 6-11). The episode is a crucial one, because the Philistine's decision freed David from the necessity of fighting against Israel. Had he done so he surely could never have become king. Thus, even though the Historian never mentioned the Lord, he clearly saw this decision as part of God's activity!

A question with two meanings (29:1-5).—Although the Israelite forces were still miles away from Aphek at Jezreel, the Philistines made a tactical blunder that eventually caused their own defeat. The commanders suspected that David would turn on them in battle and refused to have the Hebrews in their army (v. 3). In spite of the objections of Achish, they insisted that David's forces be sent back to Ziklag (v. 4). The question which they asked of Achish has a double meaning for the Historian. "How could this fellow reconcile himself to his lord?" they asked. They thought David might "reconcile himself" by turning on them in battle! But the Historian probably meant us to understand the question differently. Had David fought against Saul he could never have reconciled himself to Israel. Once again the direction of history hinged on a critical interpretation of the situation!

An answer with a hidden significance (29:6-11).—Achish reported the conversation to David, going out of his way to soothe the feelings of the great warrior. Of course, the Historian had already informed us that David had been deceiving Achish (27:8-10), and Achish had no idea how wrong his evaluation of David was. David protested vigorously, as he was expected to, (v. 8) and appeared to give in only with great reluctance. In reality David was overjoyed at this sudden

release from an intolerable situation. So the words of Achish that
"you are as blameless in my sight as an angel of God" (v. 9) take on a
double meaning, too. This release from battle made it possible for
David to remain truly blameless. So when the Philistines headed
north to meet Saul the next day, David and his men turned south—
laughing at the gullible Achish and marveling, no doubt, at David's
sudden deliverance. The Lord had preserved David again.

David's Victory Over the Amalekites (30:1-31)

The Historian followed David's journey back to Ziklag while the
Philistines moved northward to meet Saul on Mt. Gilboa. The episode involved here is important because it once again demonstrated
that the Lord was directing the affairs of David. It also prepares the
way for David's return as king of Judah.

The Amalekite attack (30:1-6).—The Amalekites were ancient
foes of Israel (Num. 14:45) who inhabited the southern portion of
Palestine called the Negeb (30:1). While David and his men had
been gone, the Amalekites had attacked the defenseless city and
burned it to the ground. They had taken the entire population,
which consisted mostly of women and children, captive. The Historian noted that David was not exempt from the anguish caused by
the raid. His two wives had been taken captive, too (v. 5). The situation was indeed grim because there was no way to know where the
captives were taken. The people turned on David because he had left
the city defenseless (v. 6). The last sentence in verse 6 should be read
as part of the next paragraph.

Strengthening in the Lord (30:7-10).—David "strengthened himself in the Lord" (v. 6) but consulting the Lord through the priestly
lots (see also, 23:16). He asked God's guidance through Abiathar, the
priest who had served him throught his long struggle with Saul. The
use of the lots involved asking a series of questions that could each be
answered either yes or no (see 23:11-12). The priest learned the
answer to the question by casting the lots, called the Urim and the
Thummim (Ex. 28:30). David received assurances that he would
overtake the Amalekites and set out with his men toward the brook
Besor south of Ziklag (v. 9). Some of David's men, who had just

made the trip from Aphek, were unable to continue and remained at
the brook.

An answer to prayer (30:11-15).—The Historian did not think it
necessary to make an obvious note about God's role in the finding of
a servant of the Amalekites, but he clearly did not think this good
fortune was mere luck. The priest had assured him success. The finding of a slave who knew the location of the Amalekite camp was the
divine fulfillment of the oracle. The Amalekites had abandoned the
Egyptian slave to die because he was too sick to travel (v. 13). David
fed him and promised him safety (v. 15) in return for leading them
to the camp. The Egyptian slave also informed David that Ziklag
was not the only city the Amalekites attacked. Ziklag probably was
situated in the southern territory that belonged to the Cherethites.
The Cherethites were the Philistines who followed David loyally
when he became king of Judah. Benaiah was their commander (2
Sam. 20:23). The Amalekites had also raided the southern section of
Judah (30:14). Caleb's territory included Hebron (Josh. 14:14).

The rescue (30:16-25).—David and his men arrived at the Amalekite encampment at twilight and interrupted the great celebration
that was in progress. None survived David's attack except those
who had mounts and could flee (v. 17). David regained all that had
been taken from both Judah and from Ziklag, including all the wives
and children. The word of God had been fulfilled (v. 18). When the
entire group finally returned to those who remained at the brook
Besor, there was some controversy over sharing in the spoils. However, David established a precedent that remained in force to the
Historian's time that those who support the front line troops should
share equally in the spoils of victory (v. 24). David based his decision
on the fact that the spoil was a gift of God and not something which
the troops had earned for themselves (v. 23).

A significant gesture (30:26-31).—Since part of the spoil had come
from Judah it was fitting that it should be shared with the Judeans.
The Historian, however, by noting the specific towns to which
David sent gifts seems to have seen more than a simple return of lost
goods in the gesture. He implied that David's act was intended to
remind the leaders of Judah of his loyalty to them while he ruled a
Philistine city. Some of the cities can't be located now, but several
can be. Jattir, Aroer, and Eshtemoa all lie east of Beer-sheba and

south of Hebron. Hormah was probably near Aroer. The cities of the Jerahmeelites and the Kenites were somewhere in this same southern area. Thus David actively sought the support of the towns between Ziklag and the Dead Sea as he prepared to return to Judea. Even as David made this gesture, Saul, then king, was facing his last battle.

The Death of Saul (31:1-13)

The last scene in the life of Saul took place on Mount Gilboa, a mountain ridge standing at the eastern end of the Valley of Jezreel just south of the Sea of Galilee. Saul's three sons were killed in the battle. A fourth son, Ishbosheth (2 Sam. 2:8) either was not involved in the battle at all or escaped. He later became king over the northern kingdom. When the bowmen got within range of Saul, they wounded him (v. 3). Saul preferred immediate death to falling into the hands of his enemies and asked his armor-bearer to kill him (v. 4). When his armor-bearer refused, Saul fell upon his sword, killing himself. His faithful attendant followed him in death rather than leave his king (v. 5). The death of Saul and the defeat of his army caused panic among the Israelite residents in the Valley of Jezreel and in the cities just east of the Jordan River (v. 7). Fearing slaughter, they abandoned their cities to the Philistines and fled.

When the Philistines found the bodies of Saul and his sons they stripped off Saul's armor—and that of the others, too, though this did not need to be said—and cut off his head. The same treatment had been inflicted on Goliath after his defeat (17:51-54). The city of Beth-shan seems to have been in the hands of the Philistines even before this battle. It guarded the eastern entry to the Valley of Jezreel. The Philistines placed Saul's armor in the temple of Ashtaroth in Beth-shan. The word Ashtaroth is a plural form of the name of a Canaanite goddess, Ashtoreth. They displayed his body publicly on the wall of the city. And, as any victorious army would do, they sent the good news of their victory throughout their territories by runners (v. 9). The Hebrew word used for spreading this "good news" is an ancestor to the Greek word used in the New Testament for "gospel." The word *gospel* means "good news." Perhaps this episode can help us sense how the message of Jesus ought to be announced; it is the news of a victory.

One group of Israelites did not flee from its city and was not about to allow Saul's body to be humiliated for long. Saul had once rescued the inhabitants of Jabesh-Gilead from death and mutilation (11:1-11). The men of the city, situated east of the Jordan, managed to retrieve the four bodies from the wall of Beth-shan at night and give them a proper burial in their own city. Years later David had these bones reburied in the family tomb (2 Sam. 21:14). Saul may have been rejected by God, but the men of Jabesh-Gilead owed him their very lives. Their courage and loyalty gained them lasting fame—and a letter from David (2 Sam. 2:4-7).

Note

1. A. C. Welch, *Kings and Prophets of Israel* (London: Lutterworth Press, 1952), p. 78.

2 SAMUEL

David's Response
1:1-27

Even though this chapter begins a separate book in the English Bible, it is the continuation of the Historian's account of events in 1 Samuel. See the introduction concerning the relationship of the two books of Samuel. The Historian followed his normal method of alternating scenes between two locations. The scene for this chapter is the camp of David at the ruins of Ziklag (see 1 Sam. 30).

The report of Saul's death (1:1-10).—It is a striking coincidence that an Amalekite brings the news of Saul's death to David amidst the devastation caused by the Amalekite raiders (v. 8). The time was shortly after David's return from the rescue of the captives, which took place while Saul was fighting the Philistines. The runner who arrived had torn his clothes and dirtied his head as a visible symbol of grief (v. 2). The runner brought the news that the Israelite army had been routed and that Saul and Jonathan were dead (v. 4). When David sought to verify the deaths of Saul and Jonathan, the runner claimed personal knowledge and participation (v. 9). In the light of the earlier narrative (1 Sam. 31:4), the runner's story seems to be a mixture of truth and untruth. Apparently the Amalekite had somehow stolen the crown and armband belonging to Saul, but could not confess that and used the story of Saul's death as a cover. He clearly expected to be rewarded for bringing these symbols of kingship to David.

The Amalekite's reward (1:11-16).—The reward which David gave was not what the runner expected! David had the man killed because he had slain the anointed king. Throughout 1 Samuel, the Historian emphasized David's respect for Saul as the anointed king. Twice he told of opportunities David had to kill Saul which he refused to take (1 Sam. 24,26). Here, once again, he stressed the fact that David did not condone the murder of a king anointed by the Lord. The Historian was also showing, by telling of Saul's own act (1 Sam. 31:4), that this man in fact did not kill Saul. Thus there could be no question of any guilt of David in this entire affair.

David's lament (1:17-27).—David's song of lamentation was included in a collection of famous poetic works by Israel's great leaders. Joshua's prayer that the sun stand still (Josh. 10:12-13), as well as this poem by David, formed part of this "Book of Jashar" (v. 1). It is quite likely that Solomon's poem spoken at the dedication of the Temple (1 Kings 8:12-13) also formed part of this collection. Unfortunately, nothing else is known about the remainder of the Book of Jashar. The word *Jashar* either means "upright" or, perhaps, "song"; the words are similar in Hebrew.

The lament itself is built on the refrain, "How are the mighty fallen," which appears three times (vv. 19,25,27). The first part of the poem is a symbolic prayer that the joy of the Philistines will be cut short. While the Philistines immediately sent messengers giving the "good news" of their victory (1 Sam. 31:9), David prayed that the news would not reach Gath and Ashkelon, Philistine cities (2 Sam. 1:20). Moreover, he prayed that Mount Gilboa where the battle took place would wither for lack of rain (v. 21). David lamented because Saul's shield had been defiled and not treated with honor. David praised Saul and Jonathan as fearless (v. 22) and equally deserving of praise, both in life and in death (v. 23). After the long struggle to escape Saul, David's willingness to rate the king and his beloved friend as equally noble is both remarkable and seemingly sincere. He credited Saul with bringing wealth to the "daughters of Israel" who owed Saul so much (v. 24). David followed his special tribute to Saul with the refrain, and then praised Jonathan's love for him (v. 26). Surely the bond between these two men must have been deep and beautiful. A final repetition of the refrain closes the entire lament.

David, King of Judah and Israel
2:1 to 8:18

Contrary to the popular understanding of the history of Israel, David did not become king of the unified land after Saul. The northern tribes maintained their allegiance to Saul and installed a surviving son over them. David moved back to Judah and became king there. Only after a long civil war did David become king over both north and south, Israel and Judah. David's rise to kingship involved intrigue, assassination (though not by David's command), and politics. After he became king over both states, David moved to unite them religiously and politically. Clearly, the picture was much more complex than most people have remembered it! The point, however, is that God worked in that age through all of the complexities of life as he does today. To note the complex political and theological developments is to praise God more—not to hide his handiwork.

David, King of Judah (2:1-7)

David's decision to leave his Philistine security and return to Judah was the culmination of a long effort to make his return possible. He had fought for Judah (1 Sam. 23); he had fought against Judah's enemies (1 Sam. 27:8-12); he had reminded the leaders of Judah's cities of his loyalty, sharing his wealth with them even while he was in Philistia (1 Sam. 30:26). But when the time came to decide whether to return he did not rely solely on his own desires; David sought God's direction. Unlike Saul, David received an answer (2 Sam. 2:1; 1 Sam. 28:6). To inquire of God meant to have the priest cast the sacred lots kept in the ephod. David's priest was Abiathar, the last in the ancient line of Eli (1 Sam. 22:20; 23:6). Although he is not named here, his presence is understood. God's word was available to David. By the process of elimination David decided that it was the Lord's will for him to return to Hebron. Hebron was roughly midway between Jerusalem and Beersheba on the map. It seems to have dominated the South then, as it does today. David moved his wives, both of whom were from the southern area, there, thus making Hebron an official residence. His army of six hundred men and their families moved with him (1 Sam. 23:13). Such a mass movement must have involved either Philistine approval or opposition. Since no opposition is apparent scholars assume that David's move pleased the Philistines. Perhaps, since they thought he was loyal to them, they viewed this as a victory for them, but it was not.

The "men of Judah," who made David king, were the leaders of the southern state only. They acted independently of the northern tribes (2 Sam. 2:4). It is important to notice that both halves of the nation had the right to choose their own king. One of David's first acts as king involved sending a message to the Northern Kingdom, both literally and symbolically (v. 5). He sent the news of his kingship in the south to the men who had risked their lives to reclaim the body of their king (1 Sam. 31:11), and he *praised* their loyalty to Saul. He also offered to reward them ("do good to you," v. 6), but, of course, at that point his authority did not extend to them! So his offer implied that a king was available in the south (v. 7) who would be good for them too! This was David's first overture to the loyal followers of Saul.

Ishbosheth, King of Israel (2:8-11)

Saul and his three sons died on Mount Gilboa (1 Sam. 31:8). An earlier reference mentioned only three sons of Saul (1 Sam. 14:49); however, the Chronicler knew of four sons (1 Chron. 9:39). The son who survived is remembered by three names: Eshbaal, Ishvi, and Ishbosheth. The name was originally Ishbaal or Eshbaal meaning "man of Baal," but later scribes who identified the name Baal with degraded Canaanite worship substituted the name *bosheth* (meaning "shame") for Baal. Both Gideon, who was originally called Jerubbaal (Judg. 7:1), and Meribbaal, Jonathan's son (1 Chron. 8:34), had their names altered by the same process—to Jerubbesheth (2 Sam. 11:21) and Mephibosheth (9:6) respectively. Ishbosheth survived the battle on Gilboa. Perhaps he was very young. If so his age would explain the role of Abner (but see v. 10).

Abner emerged as the strong man in the North. He was Saul's cousin and commander of the army (v. 8). After Saul's death Abner took Ishbosheth across the Jordan River—further away from the threatening Philistines—and made him king over the remaining parts of Saul's kingdom. Gilead was the territory east of the Jordan in which the new capital, Mahanaim (pronounced, Mah-hah-náh-eem) was located. Ephraim and Benjamin were the central mountains north of Jerusalem. Ashurites literally means "Assyrians," but probably referred to the tribal territory of Asher which lay near the Jezreel Valley. The Philistines clearly dominated the Jezreel Valley but may not have occupied it completely. Most scholars assume that Ishbosheth could not have been forty, since Saul's eldest son Jonathan seems to have been younger than that at his death.

The text clearly gives the respective lengths of reign as two years and seven and a half years (v. 11), but the rest of the story seems to presuppose that David took over the Northern Kingdom immediately after the death of Ishbosheth—not five and a half years later. Perhaps David ruled both North and South from Hebron for those years and until he captured Jerusalem.

Abner and Joab, Commanders (2:12-32)

At some point in the history of the two kingdoms the armies of David and Ishbosheth, led by the two commanders, Joab and Abner, met at the ancient city of Gibeon. The great pool there with its stone-cut staircase descending into it is still visible today (v. 13). Exactly what the word *play* means in this context is not clear, but it seems to be a euphemism for single combat. The twelve pairs of warriors "fell down together," killing each other with swords and giving this spot in Gibeon its name (v. 16). This precipitated a full-scale battle with many casualties (v. 31). The Historian described only one scene in detail, however, because it had lasting implications. Joab's brother Asahel chose to pursue the fleeing Abner and refused to be turned aside. When he would not stop the chase the older and more experienced Abner used a surprise technique to kill the young man (v. 23). The Benjamites, Saul's kinsmen, then rallied to Abner and took their stand against Joab (v. 25). Abner asked for an end to the battle (v. 26), and Joab agreed but indicated that he would have continued through the night had Abner not given in. Though Joab stopped, he never forgot that Abner had slain his brother. This story explains Joab's later murder of Abner (3:27). Here for the first time Joab's unpitying and methodical brutality reared its head.

The two groups separated and marched all night in opposite directions to reach their respective bases. Israel's loss reached a staggering 360, nearly twenty times that of Judah (v. 31)! But the attention centered not on Israel's grief but on the funeral at Bethlehem in the middle of the night as Joab paused to bury his brother (v. 32).

David and the Death of Abner (3:1-39)

The surprising words of David at the end of this section suggest one of the purposes of the Historian throughout this part of his work. David confessed that he was "weak, though anointed king" and said that the sons of Zeruiah, his sister, were "too hard for me" (v. 39). The implication is that David could not prevent Joab and Abishai from murdering Abner; therefore, one ought not attribute this deed to him. At many points the Historian has defended David from the charge that he was a "man of blood" by depicting Joab as an uncontrollable strong man. Indeed, David himself suffered the loss of a son due to Joab's cold disregard for his king's command. Thus this chapter and several others form an apology for the king; he did not order Joab to kill Abner or others and could not stop him! The surprising thing about such an approach is that it depicts David as the weaker of the two men while insisting that David was God's anointed!

David's children from Hebron (3:1-5).—During the years of war between North and South, David's power increased. One of the ways the Historian illustrated this fact was to list the children who shared the succession to both David's physical virility and his expanding influence. Each of the wives represented a strengthening of ties within and beyond his kingdom. Maacah (v. 3), for example, was a princess from Geshur, a land north of the Northern Kingdom (a marriage made after David became king of Israel and before he conquered Jerusalem?). The sequence of children is important! Subsequent chapters will show why each of the eldest children failed to succeed David. Only Chileab does not reappear. Ultimately the struggle for David's throne involved a son from Hebron and a son from Jerusalem, who perhaps represented the power centers from which they came.

Abner and Ishbosheth (3:6-11).—The Historian shifted the scene to the North to show the opposite development: the house of Saul was becoming weaker. The specific event that caused the ultimate fall of Ishbosheth's kingdom involved Abner and Rizpah, one of Saul's wives who formed part of the king's harem. Ishbosheth suspected that Abner was plotting to overthrow him. The charge concerning "going in to my father's concubine" (v. 7) was not a charge of immorality but of treason. The ability to keep a group of women absolutely inviolate constituted evidence of a king's power. If a rival could take a woman from that group, he had demonstrated his superiority, and such an act constituted a revolt against the king. Abner protested vehemently, however, that he had no such intention (v. 8) and may, in fact, have been innocent. He clearly had the power to dethrone Ishbosheth if he had wished. As a result of this challenge, Abner swore that he would help David take over the Northern Kingdom (v. 9). Ishbosheth was powerless to stop him, just as David was unable to stop Joab's actions (v. 11). Both kings were at the mercy of their military men.

Abner's offer (3:12-16).—Abner made good his oath. He offered to join with David "to bring over all Israel" to him. Abner claimed, with good reason, that he controlled the land rather than Ishbosheth (v. 12). David agreed to accept his help with the stipulation that Michal, Saul's daughter, be returned as his wife (see 1 Sam. 18:20ff). It is strange that David's actual demand for Michal went not to Abner but to Ishbosheth (v. 14). Perhaps this is merely another indication that Ishbosheth had no power and was forced to comply by Abner. Michal was forcibly separated from her husband of several years in a scene that suggests some of the human suffering that accompanies political negotiations (v. 16).

Abner's negotiations with the elders (3:17-19).—The elders of Israel seem to have been an official body rather than simply the older men of the cities. Abner's dialogue with them indicates that they had favored accepting David for a long time (v. 17). This is a reminder of how little is known about the political activity that lurks behind these scenes. Abner cited God's promise to use David as a deliverer as an argument for making him king. Thus theology played a role in the politics. The choice of David as king would enable the promise of God to be fulfilled. Abner negotiated separately with the tribe of Benjamin, perhaps because it was the actual tribe to which Saul belonged. With their support Abner went to see David (v. 19).

The murder of Abner (3:20-39).—Nothing has been reported about the actual negotiations between David and Abner after his arrival at Hebron except that there was a feast (v. 20). The Historian reported only the conclusion: Abner would gather all Israel to David (v. 21). The added note that David sent Abner on his way "in peace" emphasized the fact that David had no part in what followed. Joab returned "from a raid" (v. 22) and found that David had allowed

Abner to leave unharmed. This brought forth an outburst against the king (v. 24). Joab professed to believe that Abner was devious and attempting to gather information for an attack (v. 25). His suspicions may have been honest, but the reader has now learned to mistrust Joab! Once again the king appears to be the weaker of the two figures, suffering a tongue-lashing from his commander.

Without consulting David—the Historian stressed Joab's unilateral action—Joab had Abner brought back, and promptly stabbed him to death "in the midst of the gate," that is, in the rooms that flanked the road as it entered through the walls of the city (v. 27). The Historian attributed this assassination not to politics but to revenge "for the blood of Asahel." The importance of the Asahel episode becomes clearer here; it gives a convincing reason for Abner's murder apart from any plot to overthrow Ishbosheth!

David responded to this violation of the safe conduct he had promised Abner with a curse on Joab and a public display of grief. Both acts were intended to disavow responsibility for Abner's murder. David's curse invoked terrible plagues on Joab and his descendants: a discharge and leprosy (they seem to be synonymous here); death by the sword; and famine. Holding a spindle used in spinning thread suggested that one was effeminate. How these curses were publicized, if they were, is not recounted.

David demanded that Joab and the people mourn for Abner (v. 31), and he led the procession. As he had done for Saul and Jonathan (1:19ff), David composed a lament to be used on this occasion. The song stressed that Abner died like Nabal—a fool (3:33)—but lamented that it should have been so. He was not a prisoner, bound and fettered, honorably executed; Abner was murdered by a wicked man (v. 34). The Historian preserved and emphasized the lament to stress the wickedness of Joab and the innocence of David. He also noted that Israel, as well as Judah, was pleased by David (v. 37). The section ends with David's lament for himself which expressed grief over his weakness in relation to the "sons of Zeruiah" (v. 39).

David and the Death of Ishbosheth (4:1-12)

Following the murder of Abner, Ishbosheth alone stood between David and kingship over both realms. Without Abner to protect him

Ishbosheth soon became the target for assassins who hoped to profit from removing this obstacle for David. The Historian set the record straight; David neither hired them nor rewarded them.

The sons of Rimmon (4:1-3).—Ishbosheth's precarious situation after Abner's death sapped his courage and that of his countrymen. With no commander they were all vulnerable to attack, especially the king himself. Two captains of small units, Baanah and Rechab, are introduced as from Beeroth, a town which the Benjamites took over after its inhabitants fled (v. 3), perhaps as a result of Saul's expansion of his territory.

Mephibosheth, Jonathan's son (4:4).—This verse has no connection with the preceding section and seems to be simply inserted at this point. It prepares for the story of Mephibosheth and David a little later (chap. 9). Why it appears here is not clear, but it is interesting that the word *lame* introduced here plays a key role in the story of the conquest of Jerusalem (5:6,8). Did the Historian place this note here to contrast David's treatment of lame Mephibosheth with his treatment of the lame Jebusites in the next chapter?

David's punishment of Ishbosheth's killers (4:5-12).—The story of the actual assassination of Ishbosheth is difficult to make sense of in the original language. The two murderers killed Ishbosheth and beheaded him, taking the severed head with them as they fled (v. 7). From Mahanaim they journeyed down the Arabah, a term usually reserved for the dry valley south of the Dead Sea but here referring, apparently, to the Jordan Valley. The journey from Mahanaim to Hebron would have taken more than a night (v. 7) if they were on foot.

When they presented the evidence of their deed to David, they claimed to have been the Lord's instruments in bringing vengeance on Saul (1 Sam. 24:12; 26:10). But David noted that the death of Saul himself brought no reward save execution to the man who claimed a part in it (2 Sam. 1:10,15). How much less would he reward the murderer of a son of Saul who was further removed from the original wrongs (4:11)? Thus David had Baanah and Rechab executed for their crime (v. 12). The Historian told the story to vindicate David and make sure that no one thought he had instigated Ishbosheth's death. But he also told the story to explain why the Israelites came to ask David to be their king.

David, King of Israel (5:1-25)

In a swift change of scene the Historian sketched David's election as king over Israel, his capture of Jerusalem, the construction of David's palace, David's children born after he moved to Jerusalem, and two battles with the Philistines! The theme stressed in all the episodes is summed up in verse 10. David became greater and greater because the Lord was with him.

David's election by the elders of Israel (5:1-5).—The elders of Israel (v. 3), an official representative body, came to Hebron. They gave three reasons for asking him to lead them: they claimed him as a kinsman (v. 1); he had previously led their army (v. 2); and, the Lord had decreed that he would be shepherd and prince over Israel (see 1 Sam. 25:30). David made a covenant with the elders of Israel. The actual content of the covenant was not described. It would have included the specific requirements David made upon Israel in return for his service as king. The elders then anointed David king over them (2 Sam. 5:3). Note that there was no single act that made David king over all the two kingdoms. They formed a united monarchy only in the sense that both states had anointed the same king.

The capture of Jerusalem (5:6-12).—Jerusalem had never been an Israelite city. Its inhabitants were called Jebusites. The city itself was so situated that it was virtually impregnable. Its inhabitants taunted David and his troops because they thought he could not possibly enter the city (v. 6). The "blind and the lame" could defend such a citadel; able-bodied men were not even needed! David managed to storm the city by means of the water shaft—at least that is the most widely accepted interpretation of the Hebrew words involved which can't be interpreted with certainty. There was a water shaft in Jebusite Jerusalem. It was a shaft cut into the heart of the hill which allowed the residents to lower a jar to get water from the spring without exposing themselves outside the city wall. A passage had been cut from the spring back into the hill to let some of the water flow to the base of the shaft. Many ancient cities developed such a system to protect their water supply in time of war. David's challenge to his men later became the explanation for refusing to allow the lame and blind in the Temple (v. 8 and Lev. 21:18). The fortified city he captured became David's residence, and he increased its defenses further. The term *millo* refers to some part of the defensive system (v. 9). David built his palace there, too, using resources supplied by Hiram, king of the forested area on the Mediterranean coast north of Israel.

The Historian concluded this section with a summary statement that David understood God's role in his accomplishment (v. 12). It is always tempting to look for God's hand in the single strokes that cleave the seas or tumble down city walls. But this masterful report of David's rise to kingship points to the activity of the Lord in the complex and "ungodly" flow of history itself. This hand of God can seldom be detected in the moment of the events; it depends upon an inspired historian for its visibility.

David's Jerusalem family (5:13-16).—As before, one sign of David's blessing was the birth of sons (3:2ff). David took women besides his official wives into his "house," many of whom came to him as parts of political covenants. Neither the names nor the number of these wives and concubines was recorded here. Eleven sons are listed. Solomon, David's son by Bathsheba, was the fourth son born in Jerusalem; normally a son who was so far removed from the firstborn son would never become king. Much of the rest of 2 Samuel is taken up with an explanation of the fact that this tenth son of David became his successor!

The Philistine battles (5:17-25).—The Philistines did not object to David's Judean kingship but seem to have viewed the consolidation of both states under him as a threat to them. They came to challenge him immediately (v. 17). David met the Philistines at the "stronghold (1 Sam. 22:4)," probably Adullam. However, it could mean Jerusalem itself (2 Sam. 5:9). The verb "went down" implies that he left Jerusalem which was high in the hills (v. 17). Once again the sacred lots helped David determine the will of God. The phrase, "the Lord said," should be interpreted in the light of other instances where the Lord spoke through the priest who cast the lots (1 Sam. 30:7-8). Being assured that victory would be his, David attacked the Philistines at Baal-perazim, which must have been southwest of Jerusalem, toward Philistia. The name *Baal* means "lord" but also was the name of the Canaanite god. "Baal" here is a title for the lord of the Hebrews. By noting that the Philistines left their idols (2 Sam. 5:21) the Historian may have been suggesting that there had been a full revolution of history since the Israelites lost the ark to the Philistines years earlier. The next chapter tells of the return of that ark to Jerusalem by David. David thus is the opposite of the worthless men (1 Sam. 2:11) who caused the loss of the ark (1 Sam. 4:11).

A second battle with the Philistines in the same area resulted in victory, too, because David received a word from God that yielded a successful strategy and promised divine help (2 Sam. 5:24).

David and the Ark (6:1-23)

Perhaps it is coincidental that this chapter about the transfer of the ark follows so closely the account of David's rout of the Philistines in which the Israelites captured the enemy's idols (5:21). However, the parallel to the earlier story of the ark (1 Sam. 4:10-11) in which the Israelite ark was captured and taken to Ashdod to be placed with the Philistine idols (1 Sam. 5) is too striking to be coincidental. This story forms the conclusion of that which began in 1 Samuel 4. David's defeat of the Philistines finally redressed the military situation and made it possible to restore the ark to full use again.

The movement of the ark (6:1-5).—The word *again* (v. 1) is best understood in reference to the battle in which Israel lost the ark (1 Sam. 4:10-11) and thirty thousand men. David once again gathered such an army. The ark had finally been returned from the Philistines to a city in Israel called Kiriath-jearim. Chronicles identified this city with a place called "Baalah" (1 Chron. 13:6), and this identification has influenced the translation of the text here: David went up from Baale-judah (v. 2). It seems better, however, to treat this set of words either as describing the people from Judah—the words *Baale-Judah* mean "lords of Judah"—or as a reference to the location mentioned earlier, Baal-perazim (5:20). The second half of verse 2 identifies the ark as it became known when it was placed in the Temple between the cherubim (1 Kings 8:6). The house of Abinadab (v. 3) had been the home of the ark for years (1 Sam. 7:1). Uzzah and Ahio were put in charge of transporting the ark which was placed on a new cart and pulled by oxen. The fact that music and merrymaking (compare 1 Sam. 18:7) went along with the occasion indicates that this was more like a victory celebration than a solemn processional.

Joy turned to sorrow (6:6-11).—When the ark reached a spot called the threshing floor of Nacon (pronounced, Nah-cone) something happened which threatened to topple the cart and the ark. Uzzah, who was beside the ark, tried to steady it but was killed. In the earlier stories about the ark, the Lord "slew" seventy men who "looked into" it (1 Sam. 6:19), raising the question of worthiness to stand before the holy God it represented. The same sequence reappears here. The death of Uzzah raised the question of David's worthiness to bring the ark into his city (2 Sam. 6:9). In both instances the deaths which raised questions were interpreted as being due to violations of God's holiness and, thus, as direct acts of the Lord. But, as so often in the Old Testament, it is helpful to remember that the event has been interpreted, not photographed. The death of Uzzah was understood as an act of God. The result of this ominous event was that David did not bring the ark all the way into "the city of David" (v. 10). The ark resided elsewhere in or near Jerusalem in the house of a foreigner who probably served in David's army. A Gittite is a person from Gath, the Philistine city where David lived (1 Sam. 27). The ark stayed there three months before David felt it was safe to resume the transfer.

The final movement (6:12-19).—The Lord blessed the family of Obededom (how this became apparent is not indicated), and this sign allowed David to proceed once again with the transfer of the ark. Before the seventh step of the journey, this time David offered a sacrifice. He offered the sacrifice himself and acted as a priestly figure. The linen ephod (v. 14) was a priestly garment (1 Sam. 22:18). David also whirled (danced) before the Lord, represented by the ark. Sacred clothing, sacrifices, and excited movement, as well as shouting and music (v. 15), accompanied the ark into David's city. The ark had a special tent prepared for it (v. 17). While not certain, it is possible that the tent represented the ancient tent of meeting (Ex. 33:7). If this is the case, David combined two sacred objects in his new sacred area. The ark seems to have been especially at home in the North, in Israel, while the tent was associated with the South. Exodus 25 offers an elaborate description of the ark lodged within a portable shrine.

The final movement ended with David's blessing and a distribution of raisin cakes and bread to the people. Woven together with this happy experience, however, is a sad one. Michal's glance out the window—she was not part of the celebration, obviously (v. 16)—at the whirling figure of David was enough to focus all the bitterness she felt at David for destroying her family.

David and Michal (6:20-23).—Three times in rapid succession the Historian referred to Michal as "the daughter of Saul" (vv. 16,20,23). Michal criticized David because his vigorous dance had led to some exposing of his body since he wore only the ephod (v. 20). David's response involved a rejection of Michal's criticism and an assertion of his own superiority over Saul (v. 21). The exchange sounds bitter and leads to the statement that Michal remained child-less until she died (v. 23). Whether she rejected David or she simply did not conceive children cannot be determined. But it appears that this episode explains why no child that combined the two lines of Saul and David appeared among David's children. The Historian implied that even this was no fault of David's. Michal's attitude toward David led to her failure to have a child.

The Covenant with David (7:1-29)

After telling the story of the restoration of the ark the Historian skipped ahead to a time when David's wars were over and there was time to think of the construction of a Temple. The prophet Nathan counseled David against building a Temple but promised that God would make a "house," a dynasty, of his descendants. This promise brings a prayer of gratitude from David. The entire chapter prepares the reader for several things. It explains why, in spite of David's sin, he was not rejected like Saul. It prepares the way for Solomon's ele-vation, which was quite unusual since he was tenth in the order of succession. It interprets the continuous reign of David's family as based in the promise of God. And, finally, this chapter gives the reason why David built a house for himself but did not build one for the Lord—it was the Lord's prohibition that prevented David.

Nathan's counsel to David (7:1-17).—David wanted to build a sanctuary for the Lord (v. 2). The first impulse of David's prophetic advisor, Nathan, prompted him to authorize such a project (v. 3), but subsequently the prophet received a word form the Lord challenging the project (v. 5). Nathan's message to David stressed the past as a guideline. In the wilderness wandering the people met God in a tent (Ex. 33:7). Never in this long period had Israel's leaders been commanded to establish a fixed dwelling for the Lord (2 Sam. 7:7). Moreover, the lack of a Temple had not hindered the Lord from using David. He had brought David from the role of shepherd to that of prince and had helped him defeat his enemies (v. 8). (The reader who has followed the story through 1 Samuel knows that God's role in the events was far from obvious; the inspired Historian serves as the interpreter of God's acts in the complex history.)

The tenses of the verbs in the next verses can be rendered either as past, present or future actions. The Revised Standard Version makes them all future. David's name would become great (see Gen. 12:2); Israel would find a place of security (2 Sam. 7:10); and David would conquer all his foes (v. 11). The ancient promises to the patriarchs were to find their fulfillment in David. But a new element appears here too. Nathan promised that David would have that which Saul wanted desperately (1 Sam. 20:31) but did not achieve—a succession of descendants on his throne, a dynasty (2 Sam. 7:11). By the time the Historian wrote his account, this promise had become fact. Thus these verses were recorded to explain how the dynasty came to be— and why it should be viewed as divinely ordained.

The prophecy did not specify which son would follow David, but the Historian knew that Solomon was that person. Solomon was authorized to build the house for God that was denied to David (v. 13). And David's heir was promised an everlasting kingdom (vv. 12,16). Though the promise was directed toward David's son, it is clear that it applied to the descendants of David and not just to Solomon. Later generations anchored their faith in this promise to David (Ps. 89:3,26ff; Isa. 9:7). Thus when Jesus came, Hebrew people expected God to act through a son of David (Matt. 1:1). Moreover, the Davidic kings were promised that God would be their Father and they his son (2 Sam. 7:14). This hope that a son of God would again come to rule in God's kingdom also lived and came to fruition in Jesus (Ps. 2:7; Matt. 3:17). Thus the importance of this passage as a seedbed of hope for later generations is clear. In this passage Nathan also asserted that the Lord would not reject David's dynasty in spite of its sin. This promise of an everlasting love that "will not let us go," first given to kings, has been offered to all mankind through Christ.

David's prayer (7:18-29).—David's response to Nathan's prophecy ignores the original subject, David's request to build the Temple. It focuses instead on the promise of a lasting dynasty. David expressed in his prayer the same humility that he exhibited as a youth before Saul (v. 18; 1 Sam. 18:23). The king praised God for his past acts for Israel: the redemption of Israel; the driving out of Israel's enemies; the making of a covenant that established Israel as the people of God forever (2 Sam. 7:23-24). The last section of David's prayer petitioned the Lord for a confirmation (v. 25) of the promise and blessing on his dynasty (v. 29).

David's Wars (8:1-18)

The theme of this collection of war stories appears in the note that these successes "won a name" for David (v. 13). The Historian saw David's success as evidence that the Lord was fulfilling his promise to David (7:9). David extended his control in all directions: Moab, Edom, and Ammon were east and south; Zobah and Hamath were north; the Philistines occupied the seacoast to the west.

Defeat of Philistines and Moabites (8:1-2).—The words "after this" may refer to the other Philistine wars (5:17-25), or they may mean that after he received God's promise David did all of the things mentioned here. The list of his victories begins with a defeat of the Philistines. The town mentioned, Metheg-ammah, is not otherwise known. Moab borders the eastern shore of the Dead Sea. Although David once had peaceful relations with the Moabites (1 Sam. 22:3-4), here they are enemies. David's treatment of the captives (2 Sam. 8:2) may have been intended to show his mercy (frequently all captives were executed), but it hardly seems merciful to a modern reader. All defeated nations "brought tribute" to their masters annually. To fail to do so constituted rebellion. Thus Moab became a "servant" nation.

The defeat of the North (8:3-12).—The kingdom of Zobah included territory north of Damascus. While Hadadezer fought enemies on his northern boundary, David attacked from the south and captured much of his cavalry, soldiers, and horses (v. 4). The army of Damascus tried to help Hadadezer, but David defeated them, too, enabling him to exact tribute from this great center of power (v. 6). Gold and bronze booty were brought to Jerusalem as a result of these victories. These materials probably found their way into the Temple that Solomon later built. Hamath was a city located still further north, beyond Zobah. Its king, Toi, sent a special gift by the hand of his son to David after David's defeat of Hadadezer. This gift may have involved some kind of treaty arrangement with David. Hamath marked the northernmost boundary of David's kingdom. David's empire reached its greatest extent with these conquests (v. 12), extending from the far north (Hamath) to the desert tribes of the south (Amalekites) and reaching from the Mediterranean Sea (Philistines) to the Transjordanian kingdoms (Edom, Moab, and Ammon).

David's treatment of Edom (8:13-14).—The story of David's treatment of Edom appears with more detail in 1 Kings 11:14-22. Neither account explains why David's army treated Edom so harshly. The Valley of Salt is the barren territory between Beersheba and the Dead Sea, although Edomite territory normally lay beyond the Jordan. Psalm 60 also celebrates this victory over Edom.

David's administration (8:15-18).—The Historian took this opportunity to insert a list of the key people of David's reign. Most of these people emerge as significant figures later. Another list of such people appears in 2 Samuel 20:23-26, with a few differences. Joab served as the commander of the army, while Benaiah (2 Sam. 8:18) commanded David's personal guards. These men ultimately chose different sides in the struggle for David's throne (1 Kings 1:7-8). Zadok and Abiathar likewise served different claimants to the throne, although in this case Ahimelech the son of Abiathar is mentioned and not Abiathar himself (2 Sam. 8:17). Two people who served as handlers of information also appear here: Jehoshaphat who is called the recorder and Seraiah, the secretary (vv. 16-17). No clear distinction can be made in their duties. David's sons are called "priests" here but play no part in the story as priests. Indeed, the sons who do appear are not priests.

The House of David

9:1 to 20:26

Faithful to Old Vows (9:1-13)

Beginning with chapter 9 the Historian traced the tangled events that led to the fulfillment of the promise made in 7:12-13. If events had followed their normal, expected sequence no explanation would have been needed. David's eldest son would have ruled after him. But such was not the case. The tenth son of David succeeded him, and his ancestry was clouded by widely known events surrounding David's marriage to Bathsheba. Thus the Historian made it his goal to explain how Solomon's anointing actually fulfilled the Word of God. The complex story unfolds without any attempt to excuse the actions of the persons involved. It reaches its conclusion in 1 Kings 2 with the establishment of Solomon's kingship. Even in unclean things God was at work. When this complex story is read together with the story of David's rise to power, it is clear that the inspired Historian saw divine activity where few others would have dared look. And so he taught us that none of life can be merely secular and beyond God's touch.

David and Mephibosheth (9:1-8).—Another story which helps explain David's question (v. 1) appears in chapter 21. Early in David's reign seven grandsons of Saul were executed, leaving only Jonathan's son and grandson alive as direct heirs to the throne once held by Saul. After the execution of the other claimants to the throne, David investigated to see if there were others alive. David's search led him to Ziba who had served Saul in some capacity (v. 2). Under the circumstances Ziba could well have considered David's statement that he wanted to "show the kindness of God" to a surviving member of Saul's house as a ruse. He told David that one of Jonathan's sons had survived and was living in Lo-debar, east of the Jordan, but he added immediately that this son was a cripple (v. 3), implying that he was no threat to David (see also 4:4). Mephibosheth's protector was Machir, the son of Ammiel, a man who later helped David, too (9:4). (Curiously, the Chronicler [1 Chron. 3:5]

lists Bathsheba as the daughter of Ammiel; the name is reversed in 2
Sam. 11:3, Eliam.) David's first word to Mephibosheth was a word
of reprieve, "Do not fear," (9:7). David honored his vow made to
Jonathan (1 Sam. 20:15). The land which had been Saul's was given
to Jonathan's son, who apparently had thought it better to hide than
to claim the land that belonged to him. David also provided Mephibosheth with a pension (v. 7), but by bringing him into his court he
effectively prevented any attempt by this surviving heir to the throne
to mount a revolt. Mephibosheth accepted David's offer, noting his
own precarious situation; he was a "dead dog" (v. 8), a phrase used
to denote a person not worth chasing (1 Sam. 24:14) or someone who
deserves to be killed (2 Sam. 16:9).

Mephibosheth and Ziba (9:9-13).—David placed Ziba's family in
charge of the land given to Mephibosheth. Ziba's family included
fifteen sons and their families and twenty servants. The implication
is that Ziba was a man of considerable importance. Exactly what the
produce from the land covered is not clear (v. 10); perhaps it still
came to David to underwrite the expenses of Mephibosheth. The
Historian took space to introduce Ziba extensively because this background helps to understand some of the events surrounding Absalom's rebellion (chap. 16). One final note indicated that Mephibosheth had a son, Mica (9:12). It is somewhat surprising that the Historian did not mention Mica again, since he introduced him at this
point. The Chronicler speaks of his four sons (1 Chron. 8:35).

War with Ammon and Syria (10:1-19)

The war with Ammon forms the framework into which the Historian inserted the story of David and Bathsheba (chap. 11) and
Nathan's rebuke (chap. 12). The conclusion to the account of the
war comes in 12:26-31. In Chronicles the story of the war appears
without the other two accounts, showing that in all likelihood the
Historian chose to use this story as the background for his more
important materials. Thus the Ammonite war never held center
stage for the Historian, and his readers should be aware of that.

The affront to David (10:1-8).—Ammonites had been enemies of
Israel for years; Saul rescued the city of Jabesh-gilead from them (1
Sam. 11). David had had good relations with the Ammonites. How-
ever, his attempt to be proper and sympathetic when Nahash, king

of Ammon, died, aroused suspicions among the younger princes. They thought David was using his ambassadors to gather military data for a revolution (v. 3). So Hanun, the new king, humiliated David's officials by shaving their beards and exposing their bodies (v. 4). It was a rash act that David took very seriously (v. 5). Apparently he let it be known that he intended to respond to the insult with force, because the Ammonites hired mercenary troops to defend themselves (v. 6). The phrase "become odious to" literally means to "make oneself stink." It suggests that one has caused another person to treat him as if he smelled (1 Sam. 13:4; 2 Sam. 16:21). The hired forces are much the same as the ones mentioned in 8:3-8; all are from the area north of Israel. David did not send his full army. He sent Joab with a picked group of soldiers (10:7), and they met the Ammonites at the entrance to their city, Rabbath-Ammon—present-day Ammon.

The battles (10:9-19).—The hired mercenaries attempted to attack Joab from behind while he was occupied with his assault on the city, but Joab divided his group and counterattacked against the mercenaries, who promptly fled (v. 13). Joab's brother led the assault on the Ammonites themselves who withdrew within their walls when their help vanished (v. 14). The defeated mercenaries regrouped and brought in reinforcements. Shobach, the commander of the army of Zobah (v. 16), led the combined forces in the battle which was fought at the site called Helam. Helam has not been found. David's forces won the battle, which involved large numbers of chariots and calvary, and killed Shobach. This resulted in the transfer of some of the northern kingdoms from the sphere of Hadadezer of Zobah to that of David (v. 19). Apparently David's forces were not strong enough to beseige the walled capital of the Ammonites, however, for nothing is said of such an attack here. The next chapter opens with a campaign against Rabbah (Rabbath-ammon).

The Great Sin: David and Bathsheba (11:1 to 12:31)

What compelled the Historian to tell this sordid story with such brutal honesty? Surely he would have preferred not to tell it! In every chapter thus far he has defended David and portrayed the hand of God at work in bringing this shepherd lad to greatness. Why, then, did he reveal David's sin? One can assume that the Historian was forced to tell of David's sin in order to explain why the fulfillment of God's promise (7:12-13) involved the horrors he had yet to write about. Rape, murder, revolution, political intrigue—all were still to be mentioned. And all were traced by the Historian to God's judgment on David for his sin. So it was essential to show the sin that affected so tragically the fulfillment of God's promise.

The setting (11:1).—David sent his armies into the field to follow up the battle at Rabbath-ammon. David had acquired such importance, however, that he did not go personally to the field until time to actually capture a city (12:28). Thus David stayed behind with time on his hands while all the soldiers went to war.

The affair (11:2-5).—The scene is almost too familiar to recount. The houses of Jerusalem had flat roofs that were used for play and sleeping. Even today children who have no yard space play upon such roof areas in the old city of Jerusalem. As David walked on his roof patio in the afternoon, he saw a beautiful woman bathing in her courtyard. He inquired about her identity and learned that she was the wife of one of his officers, Uriah. Her name was Bathsheba; the Chronicler calls her Bathshua (1 Chron. 3:5). The impression is given that David acted immediately on his impulse and consummated the affair that very day. Indeed, only one meeting is mentioned, but the biblical narrators often compressed events. Perhaps the affair went on for some time. At any rate, since Bathsheba was just ending her menstrual period when David first saw her (v. 4), a period of weeks would have elapsed before she could confirm her pregnancy. Bathsheba conveyed this news to David, and David began to cover up his sin.

The plot (11:6-13).—David's strategy was to recall Uriah from the battle for consultation about the progress of the war (v. 7) and allow him to assume paternity of Bathsheba's child unwittingly. But although David suggested that Uriah visit his wife while he was back from the front, the warrior did not do so (v. 9). David's suggestion that Uriah "wash his feet" at home may have been a simple idiom meaning "relax" (Gen. 18:4). But the phrase may contain a sexual nuance, too; the term "feet" is a substitute, at times, for the genital organs (Isa. 6:2). At any rate, the use of the term "wash" seems to be a deliberate reflection of Bathsheba's "washing" earlier. The same word is used, although it is translated differently.

Uriah slept in the servant's quarters of the king's palace instead of going home. David had Uriah followed by sending someone with a "present" after him. These people reported Uriah's action to David. When questioned about his behavior (v. 10), Uriah asserted that his devotion to God and country (v. 11) made it impossible to enjoy the delights of home while his fellow soldiers were suffering hardship. His assertion was strengthened by an oath: "Not on your life!" The Historian has left some ambiguities in the account that tone of voice and facial expression alone could have conveyed. The normal oath would have been, "Not on my life." Perhaps Uriah's response indicates that he knew the situation and would not go home "for your sake."

David then asked Uriah to remain an extra day and attempted to get him so drunk that he could be convinced to go home, but that attempt failed as well (v. 13).

The murder of Uriah (11:14-25).—David sent Uriah's death sentence back by Uriah's own hand in a letter to Joab. In it David asked Joab to allow Uriah to be killed in battle (v. 15). Subsequently, Uriah "and some of the servants of David" were killed as they besieged the city. Apparently the deaths were caused by an attack that obviously courted disaster, for Joab anticipated that David would be angry when he heard of it (v. 20). In fact, Joab imagined an angry tirade from David which in effect would accuse him of getting so close that even a woman could drop a stone from the wall and kill the soldiers (v. 21; Judg. 9:53). But when David spoke like this the messenger was to quietly mention that one of those killed near the wall was Uriah. The messenger delivered his spiel without an angry outburst from David (vv. 22-24). Instead David spoke calmly and philosophically. The messenger may have been puzzled, but the reader can only be sickened by such callousness and hypocrisy. The Historian has managed to express perfectly the sudden change in expression that the news of Uriah's death brought to David's face. No one needs a television screen to get the picture.

The marriage (11:26-27).—For at least the second time David hastily married a recent widow (see also 1 Sam. 25:39ff). But this time God had not struck down the husband, and David's deed displeased the Lord. A son was subsequently born, but it remains nameless in the account. However, Bathsheba herself was not to remain a nameless cipher. She plays a key role later in the account of Solomon's anointing (1 Kings 1:11ff).

The prophet's story (12:1-6).—Nathan, the prophet who had announced God's promise to David (chap. 7), appeared again to denounce David's sin. He did so by describing a hypothetical case and asking the king to judge the actions involved. This same device was used again on David by Joab and a "wise woman" (chap. 14). Obviously David did not suspect his prophet's motives. Nathan's story of the poor man's pet lamb is easily detected by the reader as a trap, but David was months away from his deed and made no association between the story and his own life until too late. The story itself needs little comment. The poor man had only one ewe lamb that was like a family member, a daughter (v. 3). The rich man who had many lambs had an unanticipated occasion to need a lamb—a traveler happened by—and instead of filling his need from that which he already possessed, he took the poor man's pet. David's sense of justice drove him to anger over such blatant evil (v. 5). He had no difficulty seeing that such behavior was morally wrong when he sat on his throne; it was only when he walked idly on his rooftop that he could not see well. David pronounced the death sentence and demanded a fourfold restitution (v. 6). The story fits well as a condemnation of David's adultery, but does not parallel his murder of Uriah—who would be the poor farmer in the story.

The judgment (12:7-15).—Nathan pronounced judgment on David in two prophecies, both introduced by the formula, "Thus says the Lord," (vv. 7,11). But the words that have lived in people's memories were not the prophecies. People remember Nathan's accusing thunderbolt, "You are the man" (v. 7). In other lands a king could do as he pleased; but David lived under the law of the Lord as did everyone else, and Israel the king had no immunity from prophets. Nathan exhibited great integrity—doubtless at the risk of his life—to announce God's Word. To this day he stands as a symbol of truth telling and courageous preaching.

Nathan's first prophecy recounted how the Lord had filled all David's needs: the deliverance from Saul, kingship over Israel and Judah, "Your master's house, and your masters wives" (v. 8). The reference to the master's house and wives refers to the practice of taking over the harem of a predecessor as a sign of victory (3:7; 16:22; 1 Kings 2:22). While David did not literally receive Saul's wives as far as is known, the point is that he had all that a king could want and God had promised still more. But David had despised the word of the Lord (v. 9). Nathan condemned David here not for adultery but for murdering Uriah and taking his wife. The punishment announced by the prophet involved a continuing use of the sword in David's dynasty (v. 10). This prophecy explains the long series of deaths that preceded the anointing of Solomon.

A second prophecy begins in verse 11. This one points specifically to the rebellion of Absalom, who publicly took over David's harem as he entered Jerusalem (16:22).

David's response to Nathan's condemnation was straightforward, repentant, and honest. He confessed his guilt without attempting to excuse himself. Ultimately—remember that the Historian compresses the events—Nathan pronounced God's forgiveness and revoked the death penalty which David himself had handed down. But Nathan delivered the crushing news that the child born to David and Bathsheba would die (v. 14). Since the prophecy came after the birth, it is possible that the child had trouble from birth. The phrase, "the Lord struck the child" (v. 15) is a theological interpretation after the event—not a prophecy.

David's intercession (12:16-23).—For the seven days of his child's life David did everything in his power to save him. He inquired of God (besought God) through the priests. He fasted, to call in a special way upon the Lord. And he spent the night on the ground, perhaps in a sanctuary (compare Gen. 28:11ff). The lengths to which David went caused his subordinates to worry about him. When the child died they feared David's desperation would drive him to suicide (v. 18). But to their puzzlement the death of the child released David, and he returned to normal (v. 20). He cleaned up and went to the "house of the Lord" (the tent sanctuary?) and worshiped. Then he broke his week-long fast. When pressed for an explanation of his actions that seemed to reverse normal procedures, David noted that he was interceding for the child rather than grieving (v. 22). When death came such intercession was clearly pointless—so he stopped (v. 23).

The birth of Solomon (12:24-25).—Solomon's birth was not tainted. David and his wife produced a son whom they called Solomon (Shelomo), a name based on the word for "peace" *(shalom).* Nathan added his blessing to this event by proposing a name revealed to him by the Lord:Jedidiah—"beloved of the Lord." This small section has great importance in view of later events because it gives divine approval of this one who would ultimately fulfill God's promise to David (see chap. 7).

War with Ammon (12:26-31).—This brief section serves to complete the story that forms the framework around the Bathsheba episode. It is not necessary to assume that the war dragged on for some two years, but it may have. This section actually follows 2 Samuel 11:1 and tells how David was called to the battlefield just in time to be personally present for the capture of Rabbah. Joab did not take the honor of actually capturing the city; he deferred to David. David took the treasures of the Ammonites to Jerusalem and reduced the people to slavery (12:31).

Absalom and Amnon (13:1-39)

Amnon, David's oldest son, and the beautiful sister of Absalom, Tamar, occupy center stage in this narrative. But for the Historian, the spotlight did not shine on center stage. For him the story really was about Absalom, as the opening words indicate. For seven chapters Absalom is the focus of the story. Nathan's prophecy (12:7-12) already has pointed the way—for Absalom was the "neighbor" (12:11) who would in his own way punish David for taking Bathsheba. However, Absalom's story began not with himself but with the rape of his sister.

Amnon's plot (13:1-6).—The scene was Jerusalem soon after (?) David's move there. Amnon was still unmarried, but in love with Tamar and consumed with passion for her. Perhaps there was romance between the two, but Amnon was impatient to satisfy his desires. Jonadab, David's nephew, suggested a plausible way for the two to be alone. If Amnon feigned sickness the king would allow Tamar to come cook a delicacy for him and cheer him. The words for the foods involved are little known words which may have had a special significance not now understood. Amnon's request that Tamar come cook them in his presence and feed him seemed an innocent request and presumes a previous relationship between the two.

The folly (13:7-14).—David himself placed Tamar in jeopardy by summoning her to Amnon's bedside (v. 7). Tamar went as directed and cooked the food, but Amnon refused to eat it before his servants. He ordered them out of the house and then asked Tamar to bring the food to his bed, which she did (v. 10). At that point Amnon attempted to seduce Tamar, but she refused. Tamar begged Amnon not to commit "wanton folly"—a crime against the most basic moral values of the nation (v. 12). Tamar realized that by being alone with Amnon in his house she could not prove her innocence and thus would be ruined for life. In the Israelite world the loss of virginity before marriage would have precluded marriage forever. She begged Amnon to acquire her through marriage (v. 13). But in the end Amnon forced her and demonstrated that he was like his father; the appetites of the moment could overrule reason and decency. And what probably began as "a fine romance" ended in "wanton folly."

The other crime (13:15-19).—Verse 15 is as startling as it is possible. Amnon's fierce passion turned into sudden rejection—as if Tamar were the guilty one. One would hope that, at the least, Amnon was subconsciously projecting his hatred of himself onto Tamar! But perhaps we ought not be so kind. Perhaps he hated her simply because she resisted! Amnon does not come across as a person who should be excused easily on psychological grounds. He followed the attack by a further crime; he refused to acknowledge his deed to save Tamar. He sent her away (v. 16). Tamar's plea involves a Hebrew expression that cannot be easily translated. It seems to mean that by throwing her out (v. 17) he was both refusing marriage and placing blame on her. After she was cast out, Tamar ripped her long sleeved robe, dirtied her hair with ashes, placed her hand on her head—and uttered a loud wail of lamentation as she made her way home. (Compare 1 Sam. 4:12; 2 Sam. 1:2; Job 42:6.)

The aftermath (13:20-39).—When Absalom saw his sister he knew what had happened and who had done it (v. 20). He counseled silence on her part and tried to comfort her. But Tamar remained a "desolate woman" in her brother's household. David's reaction was one of angry inaction; Absalom maintained silence while he prepared to act (v. 22). Commentators frequently note that the compromised David was in no position to punish Amnon severely. The fact is, however, that the Historian stressed David's open anger as opposed to Absalom's silence. He did not tell what steps David took because his interest was in Absalom.

For two years Absalom waited (v. 23). Then at sheepshearing time when there was an occasion to gather all the family for a feast (1 Sam. 25:36), Absalom invited David and his sons to attend. David declined, and Absalom then asked if Amnon, the crown prince, could attend. Either Amnon's movements required the king's approval because he was heir to the throne, or, perhaps David had restricted Amnon's movements as a punishment. Once again, David allowed one of his children to be placed in jeopardy. He sent Amnon with the rest of his sons (v. 27).

The actual assassination of Amnon is simply reported, but the Historian allows us to overhear Absalom's instructions to his servants (v. 28). In this way the reader learns the details. When Amnon became drunk, they killed him, and every one scattered on his own mule. The mule was the royal steed, as opposed to the little ass which commoners used.

The scene shifts to Jerusalem, where rumors flew that Absalom had murdered *all* the heirs to the throne (v. 30). David returned to the earth where the death of his other son had sent him—this time to mourn a loss he could not yet measure. Jonadab again appears as a knowing counselor (v. 32). He interpreted for David the meaning of the act.

The scene ends with the living sons returning to Jerusalem as Jonadab predicted (v. 35) and Absalom fleeing in the other direction, northward, to the homeland of his mother (3:3).

David's mourning (v. 37) was for the dead Amnon, upon whom he had obviously planned to place the crown some day. Since David's second son, Chileab, son of Abigail, never appears again (3:4), he must have died earlier. Absalom now was the oldest living son and, theoretically, heir to the throne of David. But David had to allow him to return from exile first. The Historian noted that three years passed before David entertained that idea—and only when Joab forced his hand did he allow Absalom back at all.

Absalom's Return (14:1-33)

For the second time in this story a person tricks David into condemning himself. This story tells how Absalom, who was exiled for three years, managed to return home. The story ends with a tense moment when David met Absalom for the first time five years after the murder of Amnon. As in the Jacob-Esau episode the reader cannot tell until the last moment whether David will execute his son or welcome him (see Gen. 33:4 and Luke 15:20).

The wise woman's ruse (14:1-11).—Joab knew that David had softened in his attitude toward Absalom (v. 1). But the king apparently would not officially change his judgment without some incentive. So Joab provided the push he needed. In this case, it was a court scene in which a woman presented a fictitious story for David to decide. A widow with two sons lost one of them when his brother killed him. Family members who insisted on punishing the murderer were about to deprive her of her other son and "quench" her "coal" that was left (v. 7). Although the woman did not specify what action she needed, David quickly decided that the remaining son should not be executed and promised the woman that he would be protected (v. 11). The parallel with David's situation is only partial because, of course, David had more than two sons. But Absalom represented the "heir" who would normally inherit the throne from David. And, of course, Absalom was as good as dead in this regard if he never returned from exile. Perhaps David considered Absalom's murder of Amnon part of a movement to take over the crown. If so, bringing Absalom back involved a calculated risk on David's part—a risk that later cost him dearly. The fact that Joab brought about Absalom's return and, thus, made a serious mistake helps explain his own treatment of Absalom later (18:14).

The application of the parable (14:12-20).—Verses 12-14 drove home the point of the story to David, but they are difficult to interpret and especially hard to relate to the rest of the woman's story (vv. 15-20). The woman accused David of plotting "against the people of God" (v. 13). Perhaps she meant that David's refusal to let the crown prince return was a threat to the people who needed to be assured of a proper succession of power. The thrust of the proverbial saying (v. 14) is likewise unclear. It may suggest that David could die and, thus, would need his successor at home; or it may remind David that Amnon was irrevocably gone and that no good purpose could be served by losing another son. The rest of the verse supports the latter interpretation. God does not raise up the dead, who are like spilled water, but God goes to great lengths to protect wanderers. This saying may well reflect the Cain-Abel story, which stressed that while Cain was banished, the Lord put a mark on him to prevent others from taking vengeance on him (Gen. 4:12-16). Thus the woman argued that David should not be harsher than God!

The remainder of the account returns to the woman's "cover story," as if she had said nothing about Absalom. She explained in flattering terms why she came to the king himself (v. 17). David, like Absalom earlier, immediately sensed who was behind this ruse and confronted the woman (vv. 3, 19). She confessed that Joab's hand

was in it all. Again the wise woman acted wisely, praising David for
his acute perception (v. 20) and noting that Joab was trying to help.
The woman disappears at this point, and the rest of the story involves only David, Joab, and Absalom.

The reunion of king and son (14:21-33).—David allowed Joab to
bring Absalom back to Jerusalem but refused to restore relations
with him (v. 24). The exile was over, but Absalom was not yet fully
pardoned. The Historian chose this point to insert a description of
Absalom which would become significant later: Absalom had a full
head of hair which grew rapidly and weighed four or five pounds
when cut annually (v. 26; compare 18:9). His three sons are unnamed, but the Historian added that a daughter bore the name
Tamar: to Absalom his sister was not a desolate woman.

Absalom put up with being ignored for two years but then took
radical action to get Joab's attention. He burned Joab's field of
barley (v. 30)! He demonstrated that he was a man of action who
was not intimidated by powerful men like Joab. Indeed, Absalom's
action bordered on arrogance. He demanded a showdown with the
king (v. 32). The story comes to its close swiftly and somewhat anti-
climactically. In the telling of it orally surely this scene would have
been prolonged to heighten the tension. Absalom approached David
for the first time in five years, not knowing whether he would be
hugged or hanged. And like the father in the parable of the prodigal
son (Luke 15), David kissed his son. Had the story ended there it
would have been happier than it actually turned out to be.

The Man Who Stole Israel's Heart (15:1-12)

Once again it must be remembered that the Historian has tele-
scoped events. Some time must have elapsed after Absalom's return
before he began to court the discontented members of society.

Prelude to revolt (15:1-6).—The Historian did not explain why
Absalom decided to seize what presumably would have been given
him in due course. He appears much like his brother Amnon who
could not wait for things to come to him. Perhaps Absalom was not
sure that David would hand the kingdom on to him because of
Amnon's assassination. Thus Absalom took steps to take the rule
away from his father. He developed a royal bodyguard (v. 1) and

began to "politic" (v. 2)! Stationing himself outside the palace, Absalom magnified David's failures and offered to do better if he were in a position to do so (v. 4). The specific example given involves legal cases which people brought to David himself. Apparently there was no diversifed legal system to handle these cases. Absalom "stole the hearts" of the people and gained the public support necessary for a successful revolt.

A new king at Hebron (15:7-12).—When Saul died in battle David had made his way to Hebron in Judah, and there had become king over the South (2:4). Absalom had been born there (3:3). So Hebron was not only home territory for Absalom but also the center of power in the South. David had moved the capital from Hebron to Jerusalem, a move which doubtless angered some of the southern populace and may have helped Absalom's cause.

Absalom used worship as the cloak of his final movement toward revolt. He asked permission to return to Hebron to pay a four-year-old vow (v. 7). While this ruse immediately seems suspicious to the reader, it did not arouse David's fears, so Absalom must have chosen a suitable occasion. It possibly had to do with Absalom's full acceptance by David after years of exile and alienation. If this were the case, Absalom's treachery appears even more callous. Absalom arranged through secret messengers for the northerners to join the revolt at a given signal (v. 10). The actual events are not even described: the reader knows what happened. Two hundred invited guests, unaware that events would make them part of a revolution, accompanied Absalom. And Ahithophel, David's most trusted adviser, answered a summons too, but he was too knowledgeable to be as innocent as the other guests (v. 12). Ahithophel may have had personal reasons for joining the revolt: he was Bathsheba's grandfather (23:34; 11:3). And so the plot thickened (v. 12).

David's Flight from Absalom (15:13 to 16:14)

These chapters of the narrative belong together. They relate David's departure from Jerusalem to escape Absalom and consist of scenes showing different people and their loyalty to David. Following this section the Historian told of Absalom's war against David which cost him his life. Then, in a companion section to the one described here, David's return trip is related with special attention to the people whom he met on the trip out of town. The two sections taken together are a masterpiece of written description, using selected snatches to convey vivid impressions of the whole sequence.

The decision to flee (15:13-18).—A messenger brought David the news that Absalom had rebelled and that the tribes were accepting him. Absalom apparently had intended to march on Jerusalem and capture David before the king learned of the rebellion, but he failed in this. David quickly realized his desperate situation and determined to flee, partly to prevent the destruction of the city (v. 14). David's personal troops remained loyal to him; they are called the "king's servants" here (v. 15). As David departed he left ten concubines who were part of his official "house" or harem. These women represented the king's presence in the city. At several points later the role of such women becomes clear (16:22; 3:7; 1 Kings 2:22). David stopped as he left the city to review the troops going with him (v. 17): Cherethites, Pelethites, and six hundred Gittites from Philistia. It was no small army! The Historian described the departure in six small scenes, all of which show who betrayed David or remained loyal to him.

David and the Gittites (15:19-23).—These Philistines had served David as mercenaries. David's words in verse 20 were nostalgic, not realistic; the Gittites had been with him since his early days (v. 18). David graciously made a way for Ittai and his troops to go back with his blessing (v. 20), but they refused. The brook Kidron is the valley between Jerusalem and the Mount of Olives.

David and his priests (15:24-29).—For the first time in the narrative Zadok enters the story. As early as 1 Samuel 2:35, in the words "I will raise up for myself a faithful priest," the Historian had alluded to this person. But up to this point Abiathar alone had been mentioned (with the exception of a listing of officers in 8:17). Zadok eventually replaced Abiathar, who did not support Solomon for the kingship (1 Kings 1:8). Here both priests attempted to go with David, only to be sent back into the city with the ark. David expressed a willingness to rest his case with the Lord (v. 25). He trusted that God would bring him back to the ark, and, thus, did not take the ark with him. But David also pointed out that these priests and their sons, Ahimaaz (pronounced, Ah-him-ah-ahz) and Jonathan could serve as informers for him (v. 28). David planned to wait at the Jordan River until he heard from these men.

Ahithophel and Hushai (15:30-37).—As David and his company crossed the brook Kidron and ascended the Mount of Olives, David learned that Ahithophel, his trusted adviser, had defected to Absalom. The fleeing refugees all had covered heads and bare feet—signs of mourning—and all wept at their sad lots. The loss of Ahithophel increased their danger; David prayed that the counselor's wisdom would be turned to folly—as indeed it was, thanks to the Hushai, the Archite (v. 32). Archites lived north of Bethel (Josh. 16:2). Ahithophel lived in the South at Giloh. Both seem to have been trusted counselors (called "king's friend" [v. 37, 1 Chron. 27:33]) who were elderly at this point. David asked Hushai to remain in Jerusalem to try to frustrate Ahithophel's counsel while pretending loyalty to Absalom (v. 34). He could then relay information through the priest's sons.

Ziba without Mephibosheth (16:1-4).—The next scene occurred just beyond the top of the Mount of Olives as the group fled. Ziba, from whom David had learned about Jonathan's son, Mephibosheth (9:2), appeared with supplies and asses with saddles for David to ride. Although the text is not really clear in chapter 9, Ziba and his family seem to have been forced to serve Mephibosheth by David (9:10). If so, Ziba might have been justified in deserting to Absalom. The fact that he came with supplies surprised David (v. 2). But the real focus of the scene is on the absence of Mephibosheth (v. 3). Ziba asserted that Mephibosheth thought that in the revolution he—a descendant of Saul—might be made king. In view of Mephibosheth's defection, David gave all of Saul's lands to Ziba (v. 4).

Shimei who cursed David (16:5-14).—The final scene in the description of David's departure is clearly the most important of all, for it describes the feelings of an enemy of David, not a friend. Shimei came from an old Benjamite family (Gen. 46:21; Judg. 3:15) and, thus, was closely tied to Saul. He lived at Bahurim, which must have been close to the Mount of Olives and on the way toward Jericho. He stood on a hillside, beside himself with rage, and screamed curses at David while filling the air with stones and dirt (v. 6,13). This lonely figure screaming at a king surrounded by armed soldiers must have been driven by a sense of profound hatred. It is remarkable that the Historian included this humiliating picture. Why he did so can only be a matter of conjecture, but two motives seem clear. First, he wanted to point out that David was not willing that even such a deserving enemy be harmed that day. The man seemed so irrational that David considered him the word of the Lord whose rebuke he had to accept (v. 10). But a second motive seems clear too. The Historian recorded what many northerners obviously felt—that David had murdered Abner (3:20ff), Ishbaal (4:5ff), and all the descendants of Saul (21:6ff). David, in their eyes, was a man of blood (v. 7). As the reader looks back from the vantage point of this episode, it is clear that the Historian was concerned from the beginning of David's troubles with Saul to show that this very charge was not true! Here near the end of David's life he chose to describe the feelings of the Northern Kingdom explicitly and show them to be false once more. Any vengeance on Shimei would be taken care of by the Lord, not David (v. 12). Following this bitter account, the narration skips from Bahurim near Jerusalem to the Jordan River, a walk of some twenty miles, where the king arrived "weary" (v. 14).

Absalom's Fatal Mistake (16:15 to 17:29)

Following the account of David's escape, the Historian returns the narrative to Jerusalem to describe the events there which followed Absalom's arrival. The major episode in these paragraphs concerns the battle of the wise men for the mind of Absalom. Ultimately, Absalom chose to follow the man whom David had planted in Jerusalem as an undercover agent. That was a fatal mistake.

Absalom and Hushai (16:15-19).—As Absalom's forces entered Jerusalem, Hushai met them shouting the acclamation given a new king (see 1 Kings 1:34). Just as David questioned why some people would want to go with him, Absalom was suspicious of Hushai: "Why did you not go?" (v. 17). The term "friend" in these verses is a technical term relating to the office of adviser to the king. Hushai, who was David's agent sent back to frustrate Absalom's efforts, swore that he intended to serve David's son as he had served David. He convinced Absalom of his sincerity.

Ahithophel's counsel (16:20-23).—Absalom turned first to Ahithophel for advice on procedure. The wise elder statesman advised the young contender to take over his father's harem as a public symbol that David no longer had any power in Jerusalem (v. 21). Such a public gesture would preclude reconciliation and would convince everyone of the seriousness of the movement. So Absalom symbolically entered a tent on the palace roof with David's ten remaining concubines. Thus Nathan's prophecy came to its fulfillment (12:11); David's sin with Bathsheba had brought its revenge. The relationship between this act and the earlier "word of the Lord" gives a double meaning to the summarizing evaluation of Ahithophel's counsel. His advice was considered as good as God's word by both kings. But, in this case, Ahithophel's counsel literally was part of the oracle of God as Nathan had given it!

Ahithophel's advice (17:1-4).—The wise old counselor advised Absalom to march against David that very night to surprise him at daylight. He predicted such an attack would cause panic in David's camp and allow them to capture and execute the king himself without a battle. If this happened the followers of David would come back willingly, perhaps eagerly—as a bride comes to the home of her new husband (v. 3). Ahithophel thought the war would be over in a day with only one death and no lasting scars (v. 3).

Hushai's advice (17:5-14).—Although Absalom liked what Ahithophel said, he called for Hushai's advice too. Hushai, who was David's undercover agent (15:34), counseled Absalom to wait and gather a massive army from all the tribes (v. 11) before attempting to fight David's trained and "valiant men." He reminded Absalom that his father was both enraged—as "a bear robbed of her cubs"—and wise in the ways of war (v. 9). A surprise attack would not succeed in killing David's veterans (v. 10). Hushai pictured a massive force that could cover David's troops "as the dew" and annihilate all of them, even if they retreated to a walled city (v. 13). Absalom accepted Hushai's advice! The Historian saw in that fateful decision the activity of the Lord (v. 14), even as he saw the rebellion as the Lord's punishment of David (12:11).

David's escape (17:15-22).—Hushai reported what had happened to the two priests. They sent word to their sons by a servant girl who met them at a well on the outskirts of Jerusalem (v. 17). But as chance would have it, this secret meeting was not secret; a boy saw them and told Absalom. The two messengers fled to Bahurim, the last village before one came to the barren wasteland and hid in a well (v. 18) while Absalom's men questioned the owner about them (v. 20). By such close encounters history is shaped! Had they been discovered Absalom might well have reconsidered and captured David that very night. As it was, they reached David with the warn-

ing to flee on beyond the Jordan just in case Hushai's advice didn't
ultimately carry the day.

Ahithophel's death (17:23).—Ahithophel knew immediately the
ultimate outcome of Absalom's decision to delay. He was a wise
man! Knowing that Absalom could not win against Joab's soldiers
and that David would execute him when he returned, Ahithophel
committed suicide. The Historian used this brief scene to tell us that
Absalom's revolt was indeed doomed. Absalom's mistake would
prove fatal.

The forces gather (17:24-29).—Two scenes describe the gathering
storm. David returned to the city that Ishbosheth had used as a capital (2:8). Wealthy men of the region brought supplies for David's
troops and these items are listed. One person who helped was Shobi,
the brother of the king of Rabbah, which David had conquered
(10:2; 12:29). Apparently the Ammonites did not expect Absalom to
win and, thus, sided with David. Machir, the son of Ammiel, had
sheltered Mephibosheth until David brought him to Jerusalem (9:4).
And, since Ammiel and Eliam (11:3, 1 Chron. 3:5) seem to be the
same names, Machir may have been the brother of Bathsheba, who
was with David. Barzillai was an old and important resident of the
region of Gilead about whom nothing more is known. He appears
again later.

In the other camp, Absalom selected Amasa as his commander.
The Historian traces Amasa to the sister of Zeruiah named Abigail.
The Chronicler lists Abigail as the sister of Zeruiah *and* the sister of
David (1 Chron. 2:16-17). If the Chronicler is correct, Amasa was
Joab's cousin and David's nephew; even David's family divided its
loyalties. Apparently Absalom did not linger very long before
marching against David in the forests of Gilead where both armies
camped (17:26).

The Death of Absalom (18:1-18)

It is impossible to tell how much time elapsed before the crucial
battle described here. Perhaps there was only one major battle in the
entire revolt. The battle described took place in the forested land
near David's camp (v. 6).

David's order (18:1-5).—David placed the faithful Ittai, who fol-

lowed him into exile, over one-third of his forces. The rest he divided
between the brothers, Joab and Abishai (v. 2). Benaiah, David's
other famed commander, must have stayed with David in the camp.
David wanted to go at the head of his army (v. 2), but his soldiers
persuaded him not to go. So the king stood beside the gate to review
the soldiers as they left (v. 4). Later when the troops returned David
did not stand at the gate to receive them—an act which earned him
a stinging rebuke from Joab (19:7). As he sent his commanders to
battle against his son, David ordered them to "deal gently" with
Absalom (v. 5). It was not David's intention to have his son executed.
The Historian stressed David's attitude of mercy for Absalom.

Joab's deed (18:6-15).—As David had anticipated, his seasoned
soldiers quickly defeated Absalom's army and scattered them into
the forest. Absalom became separated from his men, and David's
forces spotted him. In the ensuing chase, Absalom's mule ran under
a tree, and Absalom's head became wedged in the limbs. Perhaps his
long hair contributed to his plight (14:26), although there is no mention of this. The soldier who found Absalom refused to kill him as
Joab suggested because of the king's command (v. 12). The soldier
suspected that Joab might have rewarded him with execution instead of silver, as David had once done (v. 13; 1:15). Joab himself
plunged three darts (not spears) into Absalom, and his troops finished the execution (vv. 14-15).

Absalom's monuments (18:16-18).—Once the rebel leader died,
the war was over. Absalom was buried beneath a pile of rocks in the
forest. The Historian knew of another monument in the valley outside Jerusalem that was called "Absalom's monument," and he
wanted to make it clear that Absalom's body was not there. The
modern tourist can see a tomb called "Absalom's Tomb" in the
Kidron Valley, but it is not either of the ones mentioned here. It is
much more recent than David's time.

David's Grief; Joab's Anger (18:19 to 19:8a)

The key question about this section is, Why did the Historian tell
this episode? He left out much but included this section which portrays a king overcome with grief and powerless before his commander. One answer to this question is that the Historian was again

demonstrating that Joab alone, and not David, was a "man of blood." Even though this scene makes David appear weak, it demonstrates that David suffered at the hands of Joab as did the family of Abner.

The bad news (18:19-32).—In the ancient world news traveled at the speed of runners. Ahimaaz, who had brought the first message to David that enabled him to flee from Absalom (17:17), wanted to carry the word of victory to David. Joab preferred to send another man simply called "the Cushite," that is to say, the African. For once the Historian did not introduce a character, and nothing is known about this runner to indicate why Joab preferred him. The only hint given is that the death of the king's son made it unwise to send Ahimaaz (v. 20). Joab may have wanted to spare Ahimaaz the stigma of being the bearer of such news because of his father's close ties to David. But Ahimaaz ran anyway.

The scene shifts from Joab's camp to Mahanaim where David sat by the gate awaiting the news (v. 24). The appearance of a single runner cheered David; if his army had been routed the men would have come home in groups. The recognition of Ahimaaz (v. 27) further raised David's hopes for good news; the man stood for good news! And indeed Ahimaaz gasped out the news of victory (v. 28), but he either did not know what had happened to Absalom or thought it unwise to deliver this news. His answer to David's specific question about Absalom professed ignorance (v. 29). The Cushite delivered the crushing news of Absalom's death when he arrived (v. 32).

David and Joab (18:33 to 19:8a).—Of all the scenes of pathos in the Bible, surely this is second only to that of the crucifixion centuries later. David wept uncontrollably as he mounted the steps to the second-floor room over the gate. His loud lament for Absalom was all agony and no poetry; it differed from his lament for Jonathan (1:19ff). Who knows how much David blamed himself for the sequence of events that began with Bathsheba and ended here? His wish that he had died instead of Absalom may imply such an association, but the Historian did not make the connection explicit.

David's personal grief overwhelmed his sense of duty; he did not receive his troops as they reentered the city. There was no victory celebration (v. 2) as there normally would have been. Instead the city was as quiet as it would have been after a defeat. Joab confronted David and accused him of ingratitude for the deliverance his army had achieved for him. He ordered David to review his troops and thank them (v. 7), threatening to withdraw the military from David if he refused. David was certainly in no position to refuse Joab's demand or to punish Joab for disobeying his order. So he went to the gate to review his army (v. 8).

The Return of David (19:8*b*-43)

The aftermath of David's victory and Absalom's death was chaotic. Rebels suddenly were without a cause and in danger of severe punishment. The Historian has used David's return trip to describe the king's treatment of these vulnerable enemies as well as his loyalty to those who had sustained him. This section should be studied in conjunction with the earlier description of David's departure from Jerusalem.

David's second inaugural (19:8b-15).—When David first became king over Judah and Israel he was confirmed separately by these two groups. Both sections accepted Absalom, but with the death of Absalom, both needed a new king. In Israel there must have been conflict over whom to accept as king (v. 9). Those supporting David argued that his past acts of deliverance from the Philistines were enough to commend him again as king. These supporters carried the day, but as later episodes will prove, there was still major discontent with David in the North.

David sent word to the Southerners warning them that Israel planned to crown him again and urging the people of Judah to crown him first because they were his kinsmen (v. 11). Zadok and Abiathar who spoke to the elders of Judah on David's behalf also had a message for Amasa, the commander of Absalom's army who was back in Jerusalem. David named him commander of the army, replacing Joab! This incredible move must have been popular with the men of Judah for it "swayed" (v. 14) them to David's side. Apparently all of Judah had had enough of Joab! The representatives of the people went to Gilgal, near the Jordan, to accept back their king (v. 15).

Shimei's repentance (19:16-23).—Shimei and Ziba were among the first to greet David when he reached the Jordan. Shimei had cursed David bitterly as he fled (16:5). Ziba had brought both supplies and an evil report about his master (16:1). Both had good reason to fear David's anger. Shimei, accompanied by a thousand men (v. 17), "fell down" and begged David's forgiveness (v. 19). He noted that he was the first of "the house of Joseph" or the Northern Kingdom (v. 20) to pledge allegiance to David. Again David's commander, Abishai, requested permission to execute Shimei (16:9), but David once again denied the request. David spared the life of Shimei (v. 23). Clearly the Historian intended to heighten the generosity of David by emphasizing Abishai's eagerness to kill.

Mephibosheth's story (19:24-30).—When David saw Ziba's master, his physical condition spoke convincingly of his loyalty. Mephibosheth had not cleaned himself or cared for himself since David had left. He must have looked and smelled awful. Apparently he had deprived himself as an act of mourning or symbolic loyalty. David questioned him about his failure to leave with him. Mephibosheth accused Ziba of treachery (see 16:3), but noted that after all David's goodness to him he deserved nothing more (19:28). David could not decide which of these two men was lying, so he divided the inheritance between them (v. 29). Mephibosheth professed no interest in the land since David had returned safely. The Historian portrays him as genuine and loyal to David.

Barzillai's reward (19:31-40).—David offered the elderly Barzillai a place in the palace for the remainder of his life, but the eighty-year-old man (v. 35) declined. He suggested instead that Chimham—probably his son—be allowed to enjoy the reward. David quickly agreed, and Chimham went with David while Barzillai returned to Rogelim, his home. David's destination was Gilgal where Saul had once been crowned (1 Sam. 11:14). The Historian noted, however, that while Judah was united in accepting David back, only half of the Northern Kingdom did so (v. 40). This ominous note signaled the continuing strife in the north over David.

Strife over David's return (19:41-43).—When "all the men of Israel" finally rallied behind David, it was too late for them to be the first to crown him king. They accused the Southerners of "stealing" David (v. 41), and, indeed, the Historian did note that David worked with the Judeans to assure that they could crown him first (v. 12). The Judeans responded that they accepted him first because of their special tribal associations, but they denied any wrongdoing. No deals had been made (v. 12). The Israelites were not satisfied, however, and pointed out their predominance in terms of tribes— ten northern tribes to two southern tribes (v. 43). They felt "despised" in the maneuvering and, obviously, were not happy with the new situation. We can't know all that was involved in their dissatisfaction, but under Solomon, at a later time, the North bore a much larger share of the tax burden because of the larger size. They apparently felt they had inadequate representation, and this feeling very soon led to an open rebellion against David.

Sheba's Revolt (20:1-26)

Before David even reached Jerusalem, a new revolt led by one of the Israelites broke out. The revolt was ultimately suppressed, but it cost the lives of two men involved in it in different ways. Even though David was the Lord's anointed, the political affairs of the nation still had to be dealt with in very human ways. The Historian has once again shown that Joab and not David was responsible for the bloodshed involved.

The rebellion begins (20:1-2).—A Benjamite named Sheba rallied the discontented Israelites to withdraw their support from David. Unlike Absalom, Sheba did not attack David or attempt to replace him as king. He led the Israelites to renounce their plans to crown David again. The poetic proclamation (v. 1) involved a call to action in the traditional language that developed during the tenting period of Israel's history. Sheba asserted that the northerners had no "portion" or "inheritance" in Jesse. He meant that they had nothing to gain from following David. The Israelites followed Sheba while the Judeans remained committed to David.

David's concubines (20:3).—The ten women who had been left to symbolize David's rule and were taken over by Absalom were treated as contaminated women. David provided for them in a harem, a guarded house, but did not resume his relationship with them. David's action was a political one rather than a personal one; the kingdom had to be refounded.

Amasa's fate (20:4-10).—David installed Amasa as commander and removed Joab from his command, presumably as punishment for his disobedience. Amasa's first task was to gather the loyal Judean troops to pursue Sheba and stop the rebellion. David asked him to have his force ready in three days, but Amasa could not get the group ready in time (v. 5). So David appointed Joab's brother, Abishai, to deal with Sheba. Abishai took David's elite bodyguard and Joab and went after Sheba (v. 7). Not far north of Jerusalem, at Gibeon, Amasa caught up with Abishai's forces (v. 8). Joab wore a sword but had concealed it with a loose outer garment. He wasted no time in using the sword on Amasa, just as he had earlier murdered Abner (v. 10; 3:30). He only needed one stroke to disembowel Amasa. The Historian told the story not to exalt the act but to expose Joab for what he was, a murderer whom David could not control.

The capture of Sheba (20:11-22).—Joab's soldiers demanded allegiance to Joab following the murder of Amasa (v. 11). The dying Amasa was removed from sight, and the troops fell in behind the two sons of Zeruiah (v. 13). Sheba gathered a group of his kinsmen and fled north to the upper Jordan valley to the city of Abel Beth Maacah. The city closed its gates and waited. Joab and his army attacked the city. A seige mound was a ramp leading up to the wall. It made possible the use of battering rams though nothing had been said earlier of such massive equipment. However, before the attackers could make a breach in the wall a "wise woman" offered to negotiate with Joab. Her use of a proverb (v. 18) points out her wisdom but also suggested that the city was willing to come to terms without a fight. She described her city as a "mother," that is, not a warrior but a civilian who desired no war. The woman accused Joab of waging a war of conquest against his own people, the Lord's own heritage (v. 19). Joab denied this charge. He explained that he did not want to annex territory or take booty but only to arrest Sheba who had led the revolt against David (v. 21). As in the Absalom affair, only one man needed to die. The woman consulted with her townspeople, who decided to execute Sheba and end the seige. Their action helps us understand why David earlier had feared to stay within the walled city of Keilah (1 Sam. 23:11). The story ends with a brief note that conveys more than it says: Joab returned to Jerusalem as commanding officer "to the king" who had sent him to battle stripped of command (v. 22). And David was powerless to change the situation.

David's new officers (20:23-26).—At this point the Historian chose to mention the new set of officials in David's "second" administration. Joab is well known. Benaiah remained in charge of David's personal guard (8:18); Jehoshaphat the recorder also remained, along with Zadok and Abiathar. Some new names appear, however. For the first time there is an ominous office of slave labor held by Adoram, a position he later held under Solomon (1 Kings 4:6, spelled Adoniram). One Ira, a Jairite from the Transjordan area, had become David's priest. Nothing more is known about this person. Joab, Benaiah, Zadok, and Abiathar play major roles in 1 Kings 1, which is the sequel to this paragraph. The intervening chapters form an appendix to David's story.

Additional Materials
21:1 to 24:25

These four chapters intervene between the account of Sheba's revolt and that of Adonijah's bid for the throne (1 Kings 1). They are generally considered to be like an appendix to the David story. Two of the chapters deal with episodes that fit chronologically much earlier. Chapters 21 and 24 should come before the Mephibosheth story (chap. 9). The other two chapters contain psalm material (compare 22:1-5 with Psalm 18) and a list of the important officers in David's army (23:8-39). Why these materials were placed here is something of a mystery. Apparently the Historian felt that they needed to be preserved, even if not in the main section where they belonged. The last chapter prepares for the building of the Temple and probably was placed just before the Solomon material for that reason.

Vengeance and the House of Saul (21:1-14)

Chapter 21 contains a gruesome episode that probably occurred soon after David became king. It also has several notes about battles with the Philistines that seem to portray an aging David, even though the Philistine wars came early in David's reign.

The execution of Saul's descendants (21:1-9).—At some point in David's reign the crops failed for three consecutive years. The food supply must have become very low; the situation was desperate. So David asked God to indicate the cause of the failures. The connection between nature and God's judgment was assumed (note Amos 4:6-12). To "seek the face of God" (v. 1) was to approach God with a request for an oracle (see Isa. 24:6; 27:8).

The answer David received indicated that actions of Saul against the Gibeonites had caused the judgment of God. "Bloodguilt" indicates guilt for murder (Ex. 22:2; 1 Sam. 25:33). Although the Bible does not mention such acts, Saul must have tried to exterminate the Gibeonites with whom Joshua had made a covenant (v. 2; Josh. 9:3-15). This answer to David's inquiry cleared David himself of causing the famine and also explained why he did not keep his word given to Saul (1 Sam. 24:21). The Gibeonites who were the offended party named the retribution required for removing the guilt. Seven "sons" of Saul had to be executed for Saul's deed (v. 6). Actually only two of Saul's sons were surrendered to the Gibeonites; the other five persons were grandchildren. Rizpah was Saul's wife who became the center of a controversy between Ishbosheth and Abner (3:7). Two of her sons, Armoni and Mephibosheth (not Jonathan's son), were executed. The five grandchildren of Saul were the children of either Merab or Michal (see the footnote for v. 8 in the RSV). Merab was Saul's oldest daughter who was promised to David, but then was married to Adriel (1 Sam. 18:19). The Gibeonites executed these seven men and then exposed their bodies without burial as Saul's body had been exposed by the Philistines (1 Sam. 31:10).

Rizpah's wake (21:10-14).—Rizpah took her stand in the summer months to protect the bodies as best she could. The harvest began in late April, and in most years there is no rain all summer. Rizpah's long vigil over the bodies of her sons made a deep impression on the Historian and also upon David. David ended her long vigil by burying the bones together with those of Saul and Jonathan (vv. 13-14). The famine ended then too!

War with the Philistines (21:15-22)

David's close call (21:15-17).—David's wars with the Philistines seem to have come early in his reign, but in this case David is clearly an older king. When he faced the enemy in battle he grew weary (v. 15) and had to be rescued by Abishai, Joab's brother (v. 17). This close call led the soldiers to insist that David no longer go into battle personally. The same motif occurred in the story of Absalom's revolt (18:3; see also 11:1). The enemy in this case was another warrior similar to Goliath named Ishbi-benob. The weight of the spear indicates that he was a large man. The note that he descended from the giants makes the same point (v. 16).

Other memorable victories (21:18-22).—Three other "giants" who fell before David's warriors stuck in Israel's memory, but only two names were remembered: Saph and Goliath (see the commentary on 1 Chron. 20:5 in relation to the identity of this Goliath). The Israelite heroes were Sibbecai (1 Chron. 11:29; 27:11), Elhanan (same as the son of Dodo of Bethlehem, 2 Sam. 23:24; 1 Chron. 11:12?) and David's nephew, Jonathan (23:32?). There may have been similar accounts for each of the "thirty" warriors whose names appear in chapter 23 (vv. 24-39). These people had earned the right to be remembered by heroic action.

David's Psalm of Praise (22:1-51)

David's psalm recorded here is a virtual duplicate of Psalm 18. There are some small differences; compare, for example, Psalm 18:1-2 with verses 2 and 3. Some other differences in the spelling of Hebrew words and grammar exist too, but they do not affect the translation. The fact that this psalm appears here indicates that the Historian used the worship materials available to him as he wrote. Exactly why he inserted the psalm here can't be determined. It helps in his portrayal of David as a man of God whom the Lord had blessed. The poem begins and ends with praise of the Lord (vv. 2-4,47-51). The main part of the psalm describes the actions of the Lord for which he is being praised.

God's deliverance (22:1-20).—Although David is said to have used this psalm after the Lord had given him victory over his enemies (v. 1), the metaphors used in the psalm do not describe a single event. They are as universal as expressions in modern hymns such as "We're Marching to Zion" which seldom reflect physical progress! So the psalm speaks of being in Sheol, here thought of as the watery abode of the dead where a person could be tied up. But such imagery doesn't mean that the psalmist is dead. He is suffering. The sufferer called upon God who heard him from the Temple (v. 7) and answered (see Amos 1:2; Micah 1:2). In David's time the Temple had not yet been built in Jerusalem, but, perhaps, another sanctuary could have been thought of. It is also possible that the psalm came from a period after David and the people related it to David's life anyway. The Lord's help was not a still small voice such as Elijah knew either. Verses 8 through 16 vibrate with the activity of nature in upheaval. Earthquake (v. 8), volcanic eruption (v. 9), stormy winds (vv. 10-12), thunder and lightning (vv. 13-15) all contribute their frightening power to this picture of God in action. And all this divine power combined to help the psalmist (vv. 17-20).

David's trust (22:21-31).—Unlike Christians who usually speak to God from a feeling of sinfulness, the psalmists frequently, as here, called upon God to note their obedience (see Ps. 139:23-24). The psalm David used stressed the sinless obedience of the worshiper. God's help was thought of as a reward for righteousness (vv. 21,25). God is the "lamp" who lightens the darkness for the person who is blameless (vv. 26,29). Surely if David used this psalm he did so before the Bathsheba episode!

A king's praise of God (22:32-46).—Following the section which focused on the worshiper, the psalm again deals with God's deeds. In this section the psalmist praised God for being the help of kings in battle. God is a refuge (v. 33), a steadying force (v. 34), one who both protects like a shield (v. 36) and helps trained arms to use the bow (v. 35). Through God's help the enemies were routed (v. 41) and the king crushed his foes. People from far away were frightened into obedience because of the great victory (vv. 44-46). Throughout the book of Samuel victory and defeat have been attributed to the Lord's help. Israelites believed that God was active in their affairs.

Concluding praise (22:47-51).—In stately language the psalmist praises his "rock," who gave him victory. He promised to sing praises publicly because of the triumphs he had known. While a Christian senses immediately that faith in God can't be related only to the moments of victory, the psalm reminds us that life's good moments at least ought to move us to praise.

A Psalm About David's Rule (23:1-7)

Both Jacob (Gen. 48:21 to 49:27) and Moses (Deut. 33:1) left a "last word" in the memory of their descendants. The Historian recorded a psalm-like passage which he called the "last words" of David, although as the text now stands these are not David's last words by any means (chap. 24; 1 Kings 1-2). David's words here are called "the oracle" and resemble somewhat the Balaam oracles (Num. 24). David is called "the anointed" and the sweet psalmist; both designations relate to the story of David's beginnings when he was known as a musician and Samuel anointed him (1 Sam. 16).

David claimed divine authority for the insights he proclaimed about a godly ruler (2 Sam. 23:2-3). A king who rules as God intended is as good for people as sunshine on a cloudless morning or the rain that brings vegetation (v. 4). David asserted that his own dynasty, or "house," offered such a godly rule because God had made an everlasting covenant with David's house (2 Sam. 7). Because of the special relationship God would make his rule prosperous (v. 5). Not every king could expect to rule so well. David calls such rulers worthless men whose rule is not like sunshine and rain but like the unusable thorn. In another famous passage (Judg. 9:7-15), Jotham compared Abimelech, who had seized power, to a bramble bush which had no worth in itself. The oracle is a fitting conclusion to the account of David's struggle with Absalom and Sheba.

David's Mighty Men (23:8-39)

Some of David's soldiers formed an exclusive group of superior warriors. The men are listed in three groupings, the first being that of "the three" (vv. 8-17). Next come two familiar names, Abishai and Benaiah (vv. 18-23) who were outstanding soldiers but, apparently, not remembered as among the top three. The largest grouping of names comes last (vv. 24-39). There are thirty-one names in this group as the Revised Standard Version translated the Hebrew. The total number is supposed to be thirty-seven (v. 39), but the three groups have only thirty-six names. Perhaps Joab, who was not listed, filled up the missing spot. It is possible also that a name has been lost

or that the translation has obscured a name. (See the various translations of verse 32.)

The three (23:8-17).—Three men earned special reputations in
the wars with the Philistines. Their names were Josheb-basshebeth
(or, Jashobeam, 1 Chron. 11:11), Eleazar, and Shammah. Each had
single-handedly turned the tide of battles when others were fleeing.
It is likely that the feat of Josheb-basshebeth involved an army which
he led, rather than single-handed combat. There is some confusion
about the next section (vv. 13-17) because it speaks of "three of the
thirty" while also referring to what "the three mighty men" did (v.
17). The Historian told the moving story about the water from
Bethlehem's well as one example of the work of "The Three"! The
episode took place while David fled from Saul and the Philistines
occupied David's hometown of Bethlehem (v. 16; 1 Sam. 22:1-3).
Three of David's newly gathered army overheard a wish David
made that he could have a drink from the well he remembered so
fondly. Three of his men took the challenge to bring David his drink
and in so doing took a great risk. When David had the container in
his hands he could not indulge his whim because of the great effort
his men spent to get it. Instead he offered the water as a sacrifice to
the Lord (v. 16). The story tells us a lot about David's men and not a
little about David himself!

Abishai and Benaiah (23:18-23).—Two soldiers did not claim
membership among "the three" but were remembered as especially
significant nevertheless. One of these was Abishai, the brother of
Joab. Abishai was one of the two "sons of Zeruiah" whom David
thought to be "too hard" for him (3:39). Abishai helped Joab murder
Abner (3:30) and wanted to murder Shimei who cursed David (16:9;
19:21). The Revised Standard Version footnote on the word "thirty"
(23:18) indicates that the Hebrew text actually called Abishai "chief
of the three," but important manuscripts suggest that he was chief of
"the thirty." The list of the thirty follows this section. Abishai was
remembered for his victory over hundreds of enemies (v. 18).

Benaiah is described elsewhere as being in charge of the Cherethites and Pelethites (8:18). They were foreign soldiers who served as
David's personal troops or his bodyguard (23:23). Two of Benaiah's
episodes in particular stayed in the national memory: one involved a
lion and another, an Egyptian. The lion episode was memorable for

two reasons. The day it happened was a snowy day in Israel, and Benaiah jumped into a pit with a lion, leaving himself no escape other than victory—a daring show of confidence. Like David, Benaiah also managed to conquer an Egyptian though he himself had no weapon!

The thirty (23:24-39).—Although this section begins with a reference to "the thirty" and ends with a reference to thirty-seven, there are actually thirty-six names in it. Perhaps the name of Joab was understood to be part of the list. Many of the names are just names for us because no details of their exploits have been kept. Some names have played a role, however, in the preceding story. Asahel (v. 24) was the brother of Joab whom Abner killed (2:23). Eliam (v. 34) was the son of David's advisor who betrayed him and then committed suicide (15:12; 17:23). And, of course, Uriah was the husband of Bathsheba (v. 39).

David's Census (24:1-25)

In all likelihood the story of David's census belongs chronologically at an earlier point in the account. It explains that a plague which struck David's kingdom was divine judgment for taking a census, although no clear reason is given to explain why the census was so evil. Perhaps the Historian moved the account to this place because it also explained how David acquired the spot where the Temple later stood. The story of Solomon, who built the Temple, follows this account.

The census (24:1-9).—One of the most noticeable differences between the Historian's work and that of the Chronicler becomes apparent in this section. The Historian attributed the motivation for David's decision to the "anger of the Lord" (v. 1). The Chronicler attributed this impulse to Satan (1 Chron. 21:1). (See the section on Chronicles for an interpretation of the change.) Old Testament writers did not hesitate to ascribe evil to the Lord (1 Sam. 19:9; Ex. 4:24). All human activity was ultimately under God's control (Prov. 20:24). Human activity that was clearly opposed to the will of God was explained as the result of an evil spirit from God. But evil was at times used by the Lord to achieve his purposes (1 Kings 22:22-23). In this case, David's irrational decision could only be explained as prompted by the Lord even though it was clearly against his will (vv. 10,15).

For once, Joab appears in a good light. He tried to persuade David not to take a census (v. 3). A census would have been used either to determine tax burdens or military draft levels. David's decision would have caused hostility among the tribes, especially the northern tribes that were more heavily populated. But David overruled Joab (v. 4), and the census began in the region east of the Jordan. Aroer (not the same as mentioned in 1 Sam. 30:28) was perched high above the Arnon River across the Dead Sea from En-gedi (24:5). The census takers moved northward through the region of Gad and Gilead, crossing the Jordan far to the north to arrive at Dan (v. 6). They crossed the northern region to the seacoast at Sidon and moved down the entire length of Israel and Judah, ending at Beer-sheba (v. 7). The process took over nine months and counted a total of more than a million and a quarter people (v. 9). The northern section outnumbered the south almost two to one.

David's confession (24:10-14).—In the Bathsheba episode David's sin was pointed out to him by the prophet Nathan (12:7-14), and then David confessed his sin. Here the process by which David became aware that his census was a great sin is missing. Did the prophet Gad confront him as Nathan had? Perhaps. David confessed his sin and asked forgiveness. Verse 11 may indicate that David spent the night in prayer for forgiveness. Forgiveness came, but only in conjunction with punishment. Gad announced the word of God to his king (v. 13). David was allowed to choose one of three punishments: three years of famine (the Hebrew text has seven years here); three months of pursuit by an enemy; or three days of pestilence. All three, though differing in length, constituted equal punishment. David asked only that his punishment come from God and not man because he knew that the Lord's inclination was to forgive (v. 14; Jonah 4:2).

The pestilence (24:15-17).—The pestilence seems to have been some kind of disease which swept the nation, although it is described as the work of an "angel" whom David saw (v. 17). A similar account tells of the destruction of an Assyrian army by an "angel of the Lord" (2 Kings 19:35; Isa. 37:36). David's reaction to seeing the angel working destruction was to intercede on behalf of his people

like Moses (Ex. 32:32). Verse 17 seems to fit better if it is read before
verse 16 rather than after it. The destruction had just reached Jerusalem when the Lord halted it (v. 16; compare again Isa. 37:33-36).
One particular spot was associated with the cessation of the pestilence. It was a threshing floor, a place where grain was processed
after harvesting, belonging to Araunah (v. 16).

The purchase of the threshing floor (24:18-25).—Although the
plague stopped upon the intervention of God (v. 16), the story proceeds with the building of an altar "that the plague (a different word
than 'pestilence') may be averted" (v. 21). Perhaps the Historian
thought about a permanent ending of the destruction. The dialogue
between the king and the owner of the threshing floor conforms to
the classic pattern of Hebrew custom. The owner responded to
David's desire to purchase the property by offering to give it to
the king along with his equipment and animals (compare Gen. 23:
3-16). The fact that Araunah was a Jebusite may have made his
situation different from that of Naboth who refused to sell his inheritance to Ahab (1 Kings 21:3). David paid the full price for the
land and the oxen; then he built the altar and sacrificed the oxen,
thus averting the plague. According to the Chronicler, this threshing
floor became the site of the Temple built by Solomon (1 Chron. 22:1).

1 CHRONICLES

Introduction

The book of 1 Chronicles is forbidding to the general reader. The lists and genealogies of this book must seem to the casual reader like a barren desert indeed. There seems to be so little spiritual food here that the prudent traveler devises routes that pass it by for greener pastures. But deserts are only barren and forbidding to those who do not know them well and can't appreciate the interplay of all the parts of the environment! And so it is with 1 Chronicles. If one wishes to feed here on the Word of God, however, it is helpful to have a Moses who can identify the edible parts for us and relate them to God's Word (Ex. 16:15)!

Name

The two books of Chronicles were originally one book, as were Samuel and Kings. Since the fifteenth century it has been divided into two books. The Hebrew name of this book means "Daily Matters" or "The Affairs of the Days." Very early, however, Greek-speaking Jews gave it a title which meant "The Things Omitted." This Greek title related 1 Chronicles to the books of Samuel, treating 1 Chronicles as a supplement to the other history. From about the fifth century, this book has had a title which translates into English as "Chronicles." This title suggests that 1 Chronicles has to do with a chronological account of events. None of the titles used for this work describes its nature fully; all capture part of its purpose. As we shall see, 1 Chronicles interprets history as well as records it.

Date and Background

Several elements in 1 Chronicles (and 2 Chronicles, which is part of the same work) point to a date of approximately 400 BC for this book. The genealogies in the last nine chapters, especially one list of Solomon's descendants (3:10-24), trace families for four generations after Zerubbabel. Zerubbabel was active in Jerusalem about 520

BC. This genealogy, therefore, demands a date of at least 450 BC
with some time beyond that, since the author seems to look back at
this generation.

In terms of biblical history, then, Chronicles is a post-exilic book.
It appeared long after the Jews had returned from the Babylonian
captivity. The Temple, restored by 515 BC, was a central part of the
author's life. Remembering when the Chronicler lived helps make
his work more meaningful. He was six hundred years removed from
David's time, yet David was clearly the most important figure in all
of Israel's history for this theologian. Remember, also, however, that
the materials in Chronicles were, for the most part, either contem-
porary with or directly descended from the accounts in Samuel and
Kings. The Chronicler did not write a *different* history of Israel; he
wrote a *new* history of Israel using the old, old story. The Historian
who wrote Samuel proved that God, was, indeed, at work in David's
life. He told of an everlasting covenant which God made with
David's dynasty, making it the only legitimate line of kings (2 Sam.
7). Years after the Historian first wrote, the Babylonians captured
Jerusalem, and ended the Davidic dynasty. As Psalm 137 shows,
many Hebrews felt that their world had completely fallen apart.
How could God be trusted if his everlasting covenant could be shat-
tered by Babylonians? Prophets such as Jeremiah and Ezekiel helped
the people see that God had not abandoned them. The Chronicler,
continuing this ministry to the nation, sought to reinterpret the
David story to show that the eternal covenant still existed even
though kings had been replaced by priests. He stressed the crucial
link between the old and the new—David's role in making the
Temple possible and shaping the worship life of Israel. In a sense,
the Chronicler argued that David was still there whenever the
Levites led in worship and song. No one can know for sure just how
much the Chronicler's account contributed to Israel's restoration.
His remarkable picture of David was certainly a major factor in
causing the people of Jesus' day to expect God to continue working
through David's line (Matt. 1:1,20).

Content and Theology

The first nine chapters of 1 Chronicles are lists and genealogies,
but there is a reason for giving such barebones treatment to the pre-
Davidic history. They indicate that the Chronicler knew about all

the earlier history but did not intend to deal with it. All of that history became mere introduction to David's story. Chapter 10 begins the full treatment of Israel's history, although the Chronicler still used many lists and some genealogies after this point. The scope of the history reaches from David's kingship to the crowning of Solomon and David's death. You should remember, however, that the story really extended much further, because the division between the two books was not intended by the Chronicler.

This arrangement of materials shows unmistakably that God acted in a special way in David's time. The Chronicler passed by the creation accounts, the patriarchs, the deliverance from Egypt, the wilderness wandering, Mt. Sinai and the giving of the Law, the conquest of Canaan, the period of the judges, and most of Saul's story—all to get to David immediately.

A further conviction which can be seen clearly is that God, through David, had made a way for his people to approach him. The Temple and the worship life of Israel were divine gifts—grace—which proved that God had not forgotten his covenant. The Levitical singers, like the prophets of old, were God's appointed servants who could lead the nation to the throne of grace.

As you may be able to detect, seeming deserts have food to sustain the pilgrim, if the pilgrim seeks it properly. First Chronicles is certainly not a theologically barren wasteland.

Genealogies and Lists
1:1 to 9:43

From Adam to the Exile (1:1 to 3:24)

The opening verses of 1 Chronicles can best be compared in today's world to the whirling disc of a computer as it speeds past volumes of data to get to the information to be used. The Chronicler had at his disposal the whole body of material from Genesis to Deuteronomy and did not wish to discard it. But his interests led him to zip past the age of Israel's beginnings to reach David's time. Thus the names flip by at a dizzying speed, each with a story of its own to tell. Notice that Matthew (1:1-16) employed the very same technique, while Luke placed Jesus' genealogy at the beginning of his ministry (Luke 3:23-38).

The Chronicler first traces Israel's history in genealogical form from Adam through the line of Judah and David to the fourth century BC. The person mentioned at the end of chapter 3, Anani, would have lived at least after 400 BC, possibly after 300 BC. A close reading of these lists of names will reveal that they are essentially the same as lists scattered throughout the Old Testament. In some cases the spelling of names is different (compare Diphath in 1:6 to Riphath, Gen. 10:3), and there are variations in content (Timna in 1:36 is the son of Eliphaz rather than his concubine as in Gen. 36:12). They do not seriously affect either the understanding of Israel's history or the spiritual content of the Scripture. The Chronicler reduced the earlier lists to a bare minimum, hardly pausing until he reached the tribe of Judah (2:2). Perhaps the Chronicler's genealogy of Judah helps explain the extensive treatment given in Genesis 38 to the Judah-Tamar episode. The story is necessary to account for David, for David came from that less than noble beginning. Note also the necessity of including it in the genealogy of Jesus (Matt. 1:3).

A Survey of the People (4:1 to 9:43)

Having dealt with the vast sweep of Israel's history in roughly chronological fashion, the Chronicler next treated each of the tribes in turn. He only surveyed eleven, however; Dan and Zebulun are missing, but Joseph is treated as two tribes: Ephraim and Manasseh. Some tribes appear twice. Manasseh is considered along with Reuben and Gad (5:23-26) and again before Ephraim (7:14-19). Benjamin's descendants appear in two quite different versions (7:6-12 and 8:1-40), and within the Benjamin group, the material concerning Saul's family occurs twice (8:29-40; 9:35-44).

The Enrollment of All Israel (4:1 to 9:1)

Judah (4:1-23).—Several features of this section arouse interest. Many of the names are the names of cities: Bethlehem (v. 4), Tekoa

(v. 5), Penuel (v. 4; Gen. 32:31). The prophetic reference to "Bethlehem Ephrathah" (Micah 5:2; Matt. 2:5) retains the association of the town with the mother of its founder, Hur (4:4). Some of the names reflect guilds of workers. For example, the word *Geharashim* (v. 14) means "valley of craftsman" and Irnahash (v. 12) means "city of bronze" indicating that its inhabitants were metal workers. Linen workers and potters also appear in the list (vv. 21,23).

Simeon (4:24-43).—The tribe of Simeon occupied territory south of Judah and was swallowed up by Judah (Gen. 49:7). It is not listed as a tribe in Deuteronomy 33. The Chronicler's notes perhaps reflect the process by which Simeon disappeared. Simeon did not multiply like Judah (4:27); it lost some of its cities (v. 31), and many of its people (vv. 39,42).

Reuben (5:1-10).—History has dealt harshly with the tribe of Reuben. Although Reuben is recorded as Jacob's firstborn son (Gen. 29:32) the tribe never achieved a place of prominence. Reuben was remembered as one who transgressed morally (Gen. 35:22; 49:4) and suffered for it. Joseph, whose sons Ephraim and Manasseh became tribal groups in the Northern Kingdom, like his father before him received a birthright not due him. This section reflects the historical situation in the eighth century BC when Israel, the northern section, was much stronger than Judah. Tilgath-pilneser is the Chronicler's version of Tiglath Pileser who was an Assyrian king from 744-727 BC.

Gad (5:11-17).—Gad's sons are not listed here (see Gen. 46:16; Num. 26:15-17). Instead the chiefs of the tribe are listed and the location of the tribe in Bashan is noted. The chronological note (5:17) relates this material to the mid-eighth century BC.

The transjordan tribes (5:18-26).—The Chronicler paused here to sketch the fate of the tribes that settled East of the Jordan. These tribes wrested their land from the descendants of Ishmael (1:31). The Chronicler attributed their success to their trust in God. The battle was ordained of God (5:22). Relating war to the command of God was common in the Old Testament world and formed part of a concept known as "holy war." However, such "holy war" did not usually allow an army to keep the booty as the Israelites did here (see 1 Sam. 15:19-20). The Chronicler noted here an "exile" of the transjordanian tribes in the eighth century BC. Pul and Tilgath-pilneser

are the same person (v. 26). Exile is the work of God as well as conquest (v. 26); both are tied closely to one's relationship to God by the
Chronicler.

Levi (6:1-81).—The tribe of Levi received disproportionate treatment. Obviously Levites were very important to the Chronicler; he
may well have been a Levite himself. Using a system of breaking
genealogies into symmetrical blocks (see Matt. 1), he traced the list
of high priests from the time of Aaron to Solomon's Temple (6:10)
and then carried the list to the time of the Babylonian exile (v. 15).
Thus, the Chronicler dealt first with the descendants of Levi's son
Kohath (v. 2) just as he earlier treated Judah first. Next he returned
to summarize major figures from all three levitical lines (vv. 16-30).
The reference to Samuel (v. 28) is especially interesting because
Samuel was an Ephraimite, not a Levite (1 Sam. 1:1). Apparently
the Chronicler felt that Samuel, the great prophet-priest of Israel,
had earned the status of Levite—surely a great honor in the thinking
of this writer.

Verses 31-48 reflect the decision of David to place the Levites in
charge of the worship music (25:1-8). Three chief persons are recorded here: Heman, Asaph, and Ethan. All three have their ancestry documented back to Levi himself. Note the appearance of
these names in the titles of Psalms 73—89! Apparently in postexilic
times these names designated choirs or musical organizations.

The remainder of this chapter repeats once more the priestly lineage and lists the cities where the Levites lived. In the Chronicler's
view the priests—as opposed to Levites in general—were authorized
to offer sacrifice and make atonement (5:49).

Issachar (7:1-5).—The lineage of Issachar proceeds through Tola,
Uzzi, and Izrahiah vv. 2-3 and relates the clans to the number of
fighting men produced. Tola appears in Judges 10:1 as a judge and is
called the son of Puah there. Zebulun's descendants would normally
follow those of Issachar but are missing here (Num. 26:26ff).

Benjamin and Naphtali (7:6-13).—See the quite different list in
Numbers 26:39ff. Some scholars have suggested that this list is intended to be that of the missing Zebulun because it does not fit well
with other Benjamite lists. Verse 12 may contain a remnant of a list
of Dan's descendants; see Genesis 46:23 where Hushim is a son of
Dan. The reference to Naphtali repeats Genesis 46:24. The refer-

ence to the offspring of Bilhah refers to Dan and Naphtali.

Manasseh (7:14-19).—The material concerning Manasseh's line is apparently not well-preserved. Maacah is called both wife (v. 16) and sister (v. 15) of Machir. Moreover, Zelophehad is listed here as a second sister (v. 15), while Numbers 27:1 lists this person as a male. Manasseh appears here as if he were one of Jacob's children. Manasseh and Ephraim were Joseph's sons. These tribes became the predominant elements in the northern kingdom.

Ephraim (7:20-29).—Ephraim's genealogy is similar to that given in Numbers 26:35-36 but much fuller. It includes a brief explanation of the name Beriah which relates an otherwise unknown episode. Verse 27 links Joshua to Nun and Ephraim (see Num. 13:8, 16 also). This list does not give numbers of warriors; it describes the major cities occupied by the tribe (7:28-29). Bethshean, Taanach, and Megiddo were major fortress cities guarding the Jezreel Valley.

Asher (7:30-40).—Compare the lists of names in Genesis 46:17 and Numbers 26:44-47. Notable among the names in this list is Heber (7:32). There was a Heber who appeared in the story of Deborah and Barak (Judg. 4:11) and the recent archaeological discoveries at Ebla (Tell Mardikh) have given special significance to this name.

Benjamin (8:1-28).—The treatment of Benjamin prepares the way for the story of Saul and David. This chapter divides into two parts. The first part repeats the previous reference to Benjamin (7:6) but adds to it a collection of names that do not fit together clearly. Verse 8 appears to be a brief condensation of a longer story no longer preserved; compare 2:3-4 and Genesis 38. The reference to Jerusalem is puzzling. While this city lay within Benjamite territory it was not an Israelite city until David captured it (11:4ff).

Saul (8:29 to 9:1).—The second half of the chapter (vv. 29-40) traces the descent of the family of Saul. Ner is missing in verse 30 (see 9:36), and, surprisingly, appears as the father of Kish later (8:33). Elsewhere Ner is a brother of Kish and father of the famed army commander, Abner (1 Sam. 14:50). The name Baal (8:30) is the divine name associated with Canaanite worship. Its use here (Baal, Eshbaal, Meribaal) indicates the close cultural ties the Israelites once had with the Canaanites. Later this name was taken out of the text and replaced by the term "shame" (Ishbosheth, 2 Sam. 4:1;

Mephibosheth, 2 Sam. 9:6). It is noteworthy that the line of Saul continues after him through eleven generations. Very little remains about these descendants, but clearly the line of Saul lived on even though Saul and "all his house died together" (1 Chron. 10:6).

The conclusion of the survey (9:1).—The first half of this verse forms the conclusion of the survey while the second part probably belongs better with the next section. "All Israel" is the total community of God. The document referred to is not the biblical book of Kings; it is an unknown book perhaps containing the full record of the censuses taken. As so often, however, all Israel suffered division; Judah went into exile. The concluding phrase is more confessional than judgmental; the Chronicler confessed that his community deserved its fate.

The Post-exilic Community (9:2-44)

Chapter 9 lists the people who returned to their land after the Babylonian captivity according to groups. The Chronicler groups the people as heads of fathers' houses, priests, Levites, gatekeepers, and singers. This material is much like Nehemiah 11.

Heads of Fathers' Houses (9:2-9).—The introductory verse mentions three classifications of Temple personnel: priests, Levites, and Temple servants (v. 2). The Temple servants may be descendants of Gibeonites who were enslaved by Joshua (Josh. 9:23). Heads of clans are listed for Judah and Benjamin—the territory around Jerusalem. Shilonites (v. 5) may refer to Ehpramites from the city of the ancient temple (1 Sam. 1:3) or to members of a clan of Judah, the Shelanites (1 Chron. 4:21).

Priests and Levites (9:10-16).—The reference to the "villages of the Netophathites" (v. 16) may reflect the practice of bringing Temple personnel in from their home villages to serve as in the case of Zechariah (Luke 1:18) and perhaps the Levite in the story of the Good Samaritan (Luke 10:32).

Gatekeepers (9:17-32).—The same system of housing minor Temple personnel in their villages is apparent here (vv. 22, 25). The Chronicler gives disproportionate space to these minor officials, perhaps because of a special interest in them. He traces their office back to Aaron's grandson Phinehas and notes that David and Samuel the seer (1 Sam. 9:9) made their status official.

Concluding note (9:33-34).—These verses conclude the list of officials; however, the singers are not mentioned in the body of the lists. The singers receive fuller treatment in chapters 15-16.

The Lineage of Saul (9:35-43)

This list is almost exactly like that in 8:29-38. It stresses the role of Gibeon, though elsewhere Saul's home is Gibeah (1 Sam. 11:4). Gibeon was more than a minor place remembered for its role in Joshua's time. It played a major role in the story of Solomon (1 Kings 3:4-5), and the Chronicler placed the tabernacle and the altar there in David's time. Perhaps the list was placed here to introduce the reader to Saul who appears in the next chapter.

David
10:1 to 29:30

The Transition to David (10:1 to 12:40)

The history of David recorded by the Chronicler differs significantly from that preserved in Samuel. The differences are often important because they reflect insights into God's dealings with his people. In the New Testament similar differences exist between John's Gospel and the other Gospels. Sometimes these differences make it difficult to determine the exact sequence of events or their nature. But the positive value even of problematic materials is that they give the Chronicler's witness to God's work; they reflect a believing community's certainty that a gracious God still welcomed his people into his presence and blessed them. The Chronicler's story extends at least through 2 Chronicles, but this commentary will deal only with the story of David in 1 Chronicles.

The Death of Unfaithful Saul (10:1-14)

The story of Saul's death is told only as a backdrop for the events that involved David. Unlike the Samuel account, this version contains none of the pathos of Saul's final days: no godforsaken man searching desperately for a word from God (1 Sam. 28:6); no fainted hero stretched out before the pitying eyes of subordinates (1 Sam. 28:20); no courageous king walking long night hours to be with his troops for the last battle (1 Sam. 28:25).

The story moves rapidly from a panoramic view of the battle that raged on the slopes of Mount Gilboa (vv. 1-3) to a close-up of the mortally wounded Saul begging a young armor-bearer to help him die before the enemy found him (vv. 4-5), and then back to the valley beside the mountain to capture the panic-stricken refugees fleeing from their villages (vv. 6-7). The scene darkens only to open again on Philistine soldiers plundering the bodies of Israel's dead—and triumphantly bearing away the head and armor of the dead king (vv. 8-11). Men of Jabesh-gilead whom a younger Saul once delivered from humiliating servitude took Saul's mutilated body and paid their respects (vv. 11-12).

The account closes with the Chronicler's judgment on Saul. Saul was unfaithful. He disobeyed God (1 Sam. 13:13), resorted to forbidden practices (1 Sam. 28:7), and ignored God. The last charge does not fit the picture of Saul drawn in 1 Samuel 28:6 where Saul's desperate attempts to get God's guidance were fruitless. The phrase "the Lord slew him" should be interpreted in the light of the earlier verses that tell of Saul's death in battle (1 Chron. 10:3-5). This phrase means that Saul's death was the result of God's judgment; it does not intend to describe the mechanics of that death. The same can be said in reverse for the statement that the Lord turned the kingdom over to David. The account in 2 Samuel 1—4 describes the mechanics of the political process.

The Beginning of David's Kingship (11:1-9)

Details in these verses have been treated in the commentary on 2 Sam. 5:1-10. These two passages are very similar, but they are not exactly alike.

The crowning of David (11:1-3).—The major elements that set the Chronicler's treatment apart are the use of the phrase "all Israel" (v. 1) and the reference to the prophetic word (v. 3). The Chronicler uses the term "all Israel" to include both northern and southern tribes (9:1). Since the Chronicler did not tell the story of David's rise to kingship over the southern tribes, it appears here that David immediately became king over the entire kingdom. Moreover, the

Chronicler stressed the role of the prophet Samuel (1 Sam. 16:1-3). Clearly, David's succession was a matter of divine direction to the Chronicler.

The capture of Jerusalem (11:4-9).—The Chronicler's account of David's capture of Jerusalem relates this episode to the rise of Joab to a position of leadership over David's army. The earlier history in Samuel and Kings allows the reader to see the tremendous role this powerful man played in David's administration, both for good and evil. Here he is portrayed as a man of courage who is willing to lead the attack against a heavily fortified city. Joab is also credited with building the "rest of the city" (v. 8) after David had repaired the fortress itself.

Lists of David's Key Officers (11:10 to 12:22)

The chief officers (11:10-25).—The Chronicler has chosen to present the lists of key military figures immediately after the mention of David's capture of Jerusalem. These same materials appear in an appendix at the end of 2 Samuel (23:8-39). The first group mentioned is "the three." Apparently this group included Jashobeam (11:11; called Josheb-basshebeth in 2 Sam. 23:8), Eleazar (v. 12; 2 Sam. 23:9), and Shammah (2 Sam. 23:11). Shammah is omitted by the Chronicler, but his famous deed is retained and joined to that of Eleazar (v. 14). The three are credited collectively with fulfilling David's longing for water from Bethlehem's well (vv. 13-17).

Two other men, Abishai and Benaiah, were singled out for special mention even though they did not qualify as members of "the three." Both of these men play significant roles in the story of David as told in Samuel (see 1 Kings 2:18ff; 20:10; 21:17, 1 Kings 1:32). Since the Chronicler does not tell anything of David's long struggle with the forces of Saul's son, Ishbaal, or of the struggle of David's sons to succeed to his throne, these persons play no part in his story.

The mighty men (11:26-47).—Where the Samuel list speaks of "the thirty," the Chronicler simply mentions the mighty men (v. 26). Indeed, the list here includes sixteen names beyond the list in Samuel (beginning with Zabad the son of Ahlai [v. 41], so there are forty-seven names in the list). A few names that appear in Samuel do not appear here (Elika of Harod, Shammah the Hararite, and Bari the Gadite). Other names which seem to refer to the same persons are, nevertheless, quite different. Examples include Sibbecai (Maharai in

Samuel) and Ilai (Zalmon in Samuel). Exactly how the lists came to differ in these ways isn't known. While the lists are essentially the same through the first thirty names, the Chronicler clearly had a slightly different and somewhat longer list.

Men who joined David early (12:1-22).—The Chronicler also preserved lists of soldiers who followed David while he fled from Saul and lived among the Philistines (see 1 Sam. 22:1-2). He made a special point of the defection of some of Saul's own clansmen, the Benjamites, who went to Ziklag with David (12:1-7). There are twenty-three names in this list. Other people joined David in "The stronghold," which may refer to Adullam where David gathered his forces (1 Sam. 22:1). The first group mentioned were Gadites who had been officers in Saul's army (12:14). Eleven of these leading officers, who were remembered for a daring crossing of the Jordan at flood stage (v. 15), changed their allegiances to David.

The scene that took place when some of these troops arrived at David's camp is preserved here too. David administered an oath which involved a curse on those who might act deceptively (v. 17). Amasai, who is called the chief of "the thirty" here (compare 2 Sam. 23:18), responded for the group with a vow of allegiance and a blessing (12:18). After this ceremony they were accepted into David's forces.

A final group which changed sides while David was on the way to fight with the Philistines against Saul came from the mid-section of the northern kingdom, Manasseh. As it turned out, David did not have to fight Saul (1 Sam. 29), but the men of Manasseh stayed with him.

The Chronicler remembered this period as a time when David gathered significant support from the people who had been loyal to Saul. He noted that people kept coming to David until David's troops were like the "army of God" (12:22; Gen. 32:2). Clearly, the Chronicler thought of David's early group much differently that did the Historian who wrote Samuel. There David's army of some four hundred was composed of his own kinsmen and an assortment of people who had some personal grievance that drove them to revolt.

More About the Inauguration (12:23-40)

The Chronicler followed his listing of troops who changed sides to David by describing the scene at Hebron when the Northern Kingdom accepted David as king. The scene is far different from the much simpler ceremony envisioned by the Historian (2 Sam. 5:1-5). The Chronicler listed thousands of soldiers and their leaders from each tribe who made the trip south to Hebron to acclaim David (12:38). He described a festival that lasted three days with plentiful supplies of food and drink which marked the acceptance of David as king (v. 39). And he noted that the union of Israel with Judah under David was both cause for joy (v. 40) and "according to the word of the Lord" (v. 23).

David's First Concern: To Move the Ark (13:1 to 16:43)

In 2 Samuel attention focused on David's innocence in regard to the house of Saul. The chapters following the union of Israel and Judah in the Historian's account stressed the political side of David's kingship. The Chronicler wrote for a different age, an age already convinced of David's greatness and his right to rule God's people. For this reason the Chronicler did not dwell on the political side of David's rule. He turned immediately to the religious actions which David took to establish the worship life of a united nation.

The First Attempt to Move the Ark (13:1-14)

David's first concern after the conquest of Jerusalem (11:4-9) was to restore the ark to its proper place. The entire assembly of representatives agreed that such an action had priority (13:3), so David gathered people from the far south (the Shihor of Egypt) to the far north (the entrance of Hamath) to help in the project. The ark of God had not played a major role in Israel's life during Saul's reign (v. 3). It had been captured by the Philistines and later returned to Israel. But the ark had lain virtually unused for years at Kiriath-jearim (v. 5). This town was a little north and some eight miles west of Jerusalem. It is called Baale-judah by the Historian (2 Sam. 6:2) and Baalah by the Chronicler (13:6). The ark itself is referred to by a special name here: "the Lord who sits enthroned above the cherubim." This special name stresses both the way the ark was constructed and the way the Hebrews viewed it. The cherubim were not separate beings as they are described in the book of Kings (1 Kings

6:23-28); they formed part of the lid, and the wings of the cherubim folded in toward the center of the box to form a platform on which the Lord was enthroned (Ex. 25:18-22). Because they identified the ark so much with the Lord's presence, the meaning of the ark gradually became fixed as part of its name. Thus the Israelites carried the ark in sacred processionals, and the ark represented God (Ps. 24:7-8).

David's group formed a happy processional as they carried the ark from Abinadab's house toward Jerusalem (v. 8). When they came to the threshing floor of Chidon (v. 9; Nacon in 2 Sam. 6:6), the ark almost fell off the cart, and Uzzah attempted to steady it. The Chronicler said that the Lord "smote him," but this statement needs to be compared to a similar one earlier (10:14). The Chronicler clearly knew that Saul killed himself with his own sword (10:14), but he interpreted this act as a fulfillment of the Lord's will. The point is that the words "he smote him" do not necessarily describe the physical cause of Uzzah's death! It is an interpretation of the fact that Uzzah died when he put his hand on the ark.

David's reaction to the death of Uzzah was one of fear and anger (vv. 11-12). Since he interpreted Uzzah's death as a sign of God's displeasure, the processional of the ark was halted. David placed the ark in the house of a Gittite—a person from Gath in the Philistine territory—named Obed-edom. This man may have been one of the loyal soldiers who followed David when he left Ziklag and moved back to Judah. The fact that Obed-edom's house prospered and suffered no ill effects from the ark's presence encouraged David to continue the trip. For some reason the Chronicler did not continue the story of the ark's movement to Jerusalem immediately. The story begins again in chapter 15.

The Consolidation of Power (14:1-17)

Three aspects of David's reign serve to underscore David's success as a king. The first of these is the note that Hiram, king of the powerful city of Tyre, assisted David in the building of his "house" (v. 1). Such a powerful king would not have entered into a relationship with David unless he considered David a significant king. This served as a sign to David that the Lord had indeed established him on his throne (v. 2).

The second aspect of David's reign used to indicate God's blessing on David was that of his family. The birth of numerous children indicated the blessing of God. The names of David's children appear in three places and vary in spelling and in the number of names (1 Chron. 3:5-8; 14:3-7; and 2 Sam. 5:14-16). The first four of these children were Bathsheba's (1 Chron. 3:5; Bathsheba is called Bathshua here). This information is surprising because Solomon was the second child born to David and Bathsheba according to the Historian (2 Sam. 12:24). The first child died without being named. Nothing more is known about David's children other than Solomon.

The third aspect of David's reign noted by the Chronicler was his military success. The two accounts here of victories over the Philistines are almost identical to the ones in 2 Samuel 5:17-25. See the interpretation of these verses given earlier. A few differences need to be recognized, however. The Chronicler tended to use the word *God* when he wrote about divine activity (1 Chron. 14:10). The Historian used the word *Lord* in 2 Samuel 5:19. The two writers used different towns to describe the extent of David's victory: Geba (2 Sam. 5:25) and Gibeon (14:16). The two names are very close and tended to be confused in other passages too. The Chronicler also noted that David had the captured Philistine idols burned (v. 12). And, finally, the Chronicler added a concluding note stressing the spread of the fame of David and the respect that other nations paid him (v. 17).

The Transfer of the Ark by Levites (15:1 to 16:43)

The Chronicler reported the final transfer of the ark quite differently than the Historian (2 Sam. 6). He gave great attention to priests and Levites who carried the ark and stressed the absence of these religious figures in the first attempt (15:1-24). In addition the Chronicler left out the dialogue between David and Michal although he retained the note about Michal looking at the scene from her window (v. 29).

The need for proper ministers (15:1-24).—The law of Deuteronomy had granted the task of carrying the ark to Levites, that is, descendants of the tribe of Levi (Deut. 10:8). The Historian who wrote the Samuel version of this story did not mention the Levites. The Chronicler, however, placed great emphasis on this law and reported that David did too (15:2). David decided that the death of Uzzah occurred because the Levites had not carried the ark as the law required (v. 13). So David gathered a proper assembly and appointed the two priests, Zadok and Abiathar, and six Levites with all their "brethren" to carry the ark properly (v. 11).

The Levites were also responsible for music and singing. Heman, Asaph, and Ethan played the cymbals (v. 19). Another group used harps (v. 20), while a third group assisted the service with lyres. The words Alamoth and Sheminith (vv. 20:21) may refer to specific rhythms or to special kinds of instruments. They can't be defined further. One other group, called "gatekeepers," assisted. They formed part of the ministering team. Perhaps they are related to the famous "doorkeepers" of Psalm 84:10.

The fact that the Chronicler placed such stress on the proper ritual for moving the ark and the use of sacred persons indicates that these things were important to him. It is plausible that such people as Levites and gatekeepers still performed specified rituals in the day of the Chronicler. If so his account underscored their importance. Since Levites were mentioned so prominently by the Chronicler, scholars assume that they formed a special part of the ministers in the restored Temple!

The actual transfer of the ark (15:25 to 16:3).—David returned to the house of Obed-edom where he had left the ark and had the Levites carry it as the law required (Ex. 25:14). When no disaster struck the processional, David offered a large sacrifice in thanksgiving for God's help (15:26; compare 2 Sam. 6:13). The first steps must have been full of tension for the Levites who, perhaps, thought they might die as had Uzzah.

David dressed as one of the priests (v. 27). No one thought David was stepping beyond his proper sphere as Saul had done (1 Sam. 13:9). Motives and attitudes must have made a big difference! One person who also wore the priestly garment was Chenaniah who was "the leader of the music of the singers" (vv. 22,27). This person is something of a mystery because of the word used for "music." In the prophetic books this word means a prophetic message (Isa. 13:1; Hab. 1:1). Literally, it refers to a burden or something lifted up. Perhaps Chenaniah was the person in charge of lifting up the ark rather than a musician!

The note about Michal's action stands out in the Chronicler's account (v. 29). The Chronicler did not mention Michal earlier. Unless one knew the Samuel version (1 Sam. 18:20-29; 2 Sam.

3:13-16), this note would be meaningless. But the Chronicler placed it at this point just as the Historian had done. Perhaps the Chronicler retained the note because it reflected badly on the line of Saul. Michal despised David while he was doing a great thing! The Chronicler consistently portrayed the line of Saul as bad.

David successfully brought the ark into the city to the place prepared for it (16:1) and led in both sacrifices to the Lord and a distribution of food to the people (vv. 2-3). This service was followed by the establishment of a permanent group of Levites to minister before the ark (16:4-43).

The service of the ark (16:4-43).—According to the Chronicler David himself established the worship services before the ark (v. 4). The names of the Levites in this list are the same as those already mentioned (15:17ff). This section expands the earlier lists to indicate the kind of thanksgiving actually sung by the Levites. The psalm recorded here contains portions of at least three poems from the book of Psalms (Pss. 105:1-15; 96:1-13; 106:1,47-48). The psalms called upon the people to thank the Lord for keeping the covenant he made with Abraham (v. 16). They also urged the people to tell of the Lord's saving actions through song (16:23). In a third section the psalmists asked the worshipers to confess that "the Lord reigns" (v. 31). The service ended with an "Amen" (v. 36).

In a concluding section the Chronicler once again mentioned the names of those left in charge. Only one part of this section needs further comment. The Chronicler noted that Zadok's group remained at Gibeon, "before the tabernacle of the Lord" (v. 39). This note suggests that the tabernacle had been at Gibeon all the time the ark had been at Kireath-jearim. It also says that two separate groups served the tabernacle and the ark. This is quite a different understanding of the tabernacle from that of the Samuel account where no mention was made of Gibeon in regard to the worship life of the nation. The Chronicler stressed the importance of the "high place," the sacred area, at Gibeon. Later he recorded Solomon's prayer there (2 Chron. 1:3). It is interesting that the Chronicler stressed one law from Deuteronomy (1 Chron. 15:2; Deut. 10:8) and said nothing about the law requiring worship at only one place (Deut. 12: 2-5). Apparently the high place at Gibeon was an honored and acceptable place of worship prior to the building of the Temple.

David's Next Concern: To Build the Temple (17:1 to 21:27)

The First Attempt to Build the Temple (17:1-27)

The Chronicler's account of David's desire to build a temple for the Lord parallels very closely the same story in 2 Samuel, although there are some differences. See the interpretation offered earlier (2 Sam. 7).

The major thrust of this section is that David wanted to build a temple and was prevented from doing so only by a revelation from the Lord through Nathan. At a later point the Chronicler suggests that David's military endeavors made him unfit to build the Temple (22:8).

The Consolidation of Power (18:1 to 20:8)

Once again the Chronicler followed the older account very closely (2 Sam. 8). He omitted a verse which described David's systematic executions of the Moabites (2 Sam. 8:2) and made Abishai responsible for slaying eighteen thousand Edomites instead of David (18:12; 2 Sam. 8:13). On the positive side, the Chronicler stressed the use made of the booty captured from the Syrians; Solomon used the bronze to fashion the furnishings for the Temple (v. 8). Clearly, the Chronicler thought David was worthy of honor and sought to give a favorable portrait of him. In the light of this clear purpose, it is somewhat surprising that the Chronicler completely omitted the story of David's kindness to Mephibosheth. One reason for this omission may have been his treatment of Saul in general. He omitted nearly all references to Saul and even declared that Saul's whole "house" had died on Mount Gilboa (10:6). Thus there was no room for Mephibosheth after that point.

Chapter 19 follows 2 Samuel 10 with few exceptions. See the comment on that section. This chapter continues the description of the way David consolidated power in his kingdom.

With the beginning of chapter 20, however, the Chronicler made a profound change in the earlier account. He completely omitted the account of David's sin with Bathsheba (2 Sam. 11:2 to 12:25)! This story should come between the sentence, "But David remained at Jerusalem," and the sentence, "And Joab smote Rabbah and overthrew it" (v. 1). Perhaps the Chronicler simply disagreed with the emphasis placed on David's sin by the Historian. For him the actions David took in establishing Israel's worship life were much more significant than his sin. Another change which the Chronicler made in this section involved a reference to Goliath (20:5). In 1 Samuel 17, David was credited with the victory over Goliath. A later statement attributed the same victory to "Elhanan" (2 Sam. 21:19). The Chronicler resolved the problem by noting that Elhanan slew "the brother of Goliath" named Lahmi. The facts behind this confusing sequence can no longer be determined. The Chronicler presented these stories to stress the growth of David's power.

David's Sin: The Census (21:1-27)

Satan incited David (21:1-6).—This section offers one of the clearest indications of all that the Chronicler included theological changes as well as historical ones in his work. This same section in 2 Samuel indicates that the Lord incited David to take a census as a result of the Lord's anger (24:1). Since at a later point the Lord clearly punished David for doing this, the Samuel account seems inconsistent to the modern reader. The Chronicler has helped his readers understand this section by changing the subject of the "inciting" to Satan. Thus Satan incited David, and then the Lord punished him.

There are other differences in this section from that of Samuel, too. The Chronicler omitted the list of cities visited by Joab (2 Sam. 24:5-8). He used a slightly different total number of people counted. And, he included a note that Levi and Benjamin were not counted. The law exempted Levi from such a numbering (Num. 1:49). Perhaps the Chronicler exempted Benjamin because it was the later site of the Temple. Benjamin was also Saul's home and, historically, there may have been good reason for omitting it in a military census. The fact that Joab conducted the census suggests that it was military in nature.

God was displeased (21:7-13).—This section is very close to that of the Historian's account (2 Sam. 24:10-14), but there are some differences. The Chronicler makes it very clear that "God was displeased" with David. The earlier history omitted this statement and began with David's repentance. The Chronicler has also made the choice of punishments a little clearer. He did this by making a clear distinction between the "sword of your enemies" and the "sword of the Lord" (v. 12). This explains the choice David had to make and his answer: he preferred to experience the "sword of the Lord" (v. 12).

Jerusalem spared (21:14-17).—In this section there is a slight difference that may be significant. The Chronicler consistently favored the Southern Kingdom. Here he limits the destruction to the "men of Israel" (v. 14). The Historian had described the death spread from "Dan to Beersheba" (2 Sam. 24:15). When the angel approached the southern section which would have begun with Jerusalem, "the Lord saw, and he repented" (v. 15). Thus the Chronicler excluded the south from the punishment inflicted as a result of David's sin. The specific point at which the pestilence stopped was a threshing floor, a place where a farmer brought his grain to separate the grain from the stalks and the husks. The farmer, according to the Chronicler, was Ornan; he was called Araunah in the earlier history (2 Sam. 24:16).

The purchase of the threshing floor (21:18-27).—Once again the prophet Gad acted as God's spokesman. He instructed David to build an altar at the point where the pestilence stopped. The Chronicler thought of the vision of the angel hovering over the threshing floor as being simultaneous with Gad's instruction to David. Indeed, the angel himself told Gad to speak to David (v. 18), and Ornan saw the angel (v. 20). David did as Gad instructed him, and purchased the threshing floor from Ornan. The price paid according to the Chronicler was much greater than that reported in Samuel: six hundred shekels of *gold* rather than fifty shekels of silver (v. 25; 2 Sam. 24:24). This site became the very spot at which David's dream of a temple for the Lord became a reality under Solomon.

Preparations for Building the Temple (21:28 to 22:19)

The choice of the Temple site (21:28 to 22:1).—The cessation of the pestilence constituted an answer to prayer for David. Since this event took place at the treshing floor, David responded by offering sacrifices there. The Chronicler thought of the city of Gibeon as the appropriate place to offer sacrifices. He located the Mosaic tabernacle and altar of sacrifice there. Perhaps the Chronicler had in mind the prohibition in Deuteronomy 12:11-14 against offering sacrifice at places not authorized. Apparently he thought of the sacred place at Gibeon as the place where the Lord chose to "make his name dwell" in the time of David. Thus he explained that David could not sacrifice at that spot because of the pestilence which is here again referred to as "the sword of the angel of the Lord" (21:30). When David saw that the Lord responded to him at the threshing floor he decided to build the Temple there and place there the altar for sacrifices.

David's advance preparation (22:2-5).—The reference to "aliens" indicates a category of non-Israelites who lived in the land. David conscripted these peoples to work. Solomon later used such people in the actual building of the Temple (1 Kings 9:15-22). It is clear from Solomon's actions that the use of such people involved virtual slavery. There are many laws in the Old Testament designed to protect the "sojourner" against oppression. The sojourners seem to have needed it!

In addition to the gathering of laboring groups to work, David is said to have stockpiled supplies of stone, iron, bronze, and cedar for use in the construction of the Temple. According to the Chronicler David did all this while Solomon was still young (v. 5). The book of Samuel describes the relationship of David and Solomon quite differently. There David seems to have assumed that Amnon and Absalom in turn would become king after him. Here David is described as planning on the succession of Solomon from his youth.

David's charge to Solomon (22:6-16).—Much of this section is related to 2 Samuel 7 and 1 Kings 8; however, there is no parallel for this section as a whole. According to the Chronicler, David charged his son with fulfilling the promise which God made to him (22:9-10). He attributed his own failure to build the Temple to his involvement with the shedding of blood. This is an interesting confession since this is precisely the charge levelled against David by his enemies in the earlier history (2 Sam. 16:7). On the contrary, Solomon is a man of "peace" who brought "quiet" to Israel (22:9).

David prayed that Solomon would have wisdom and that he would keep the law of Moses. The language of verse 13 sounds much like that of the book of Deuteronomy (see Deut. 6:2; 17:18-20). Once again David's contribution to the preparations is stressed; this time, however, the amount of the precious metals is exhorbitant. Compare the one hundred thousand talents of silver mentioned with the income of Solomon, whose wealth far exceeded David's (1 Kings 10:14-25).

David's charge to the leaders of Israel (22:17-19).—In this case the term *Israel* seems to refer to the entire nation, not just to the Northern Kingdom. David pointed out to them that he had relieved them of concern for their own safety. The time had come for them to devote their energies to a constructive project. The emphasis given later to the tremendous cost of the Temple in terms of both people and wealth indicates that it required great dedication. Perhaps there was not complete cooperation among the various groups for this great project. Here David is described as encouraging the leaders of the nation to support the building of the Temple.

The Transition to Solomon (23:1 to 29:30)

The Inaugural Assembly (23:1 to 27:34)

This last section of 1 Chronicles is composed primarily of lists of various groups and their duties. However, the Chronicler introduced these lists by suggesting that David called all these people together for the crowning of Solomon. Thus these last chapters form an elaborate inauguration ceremony complete with the people involved, the prayers offered, the offerings taken and the ritual of installation. The difference between what is described here and the process described in 1 Kings 1:32-40 is startling. The Chronicler has described a ceremony befitting a monarch. While there may well be authentic elements of the Solomonic inauguration preserved here, it seems that the Chronicler has constructed the ceremony as it "ought" to have been because of his great reverence for David and Solomon.

The first verses of this section form a title. The entire section deals with the crowning of Solomon (v. 1) while the first unit in this story lists the participants (v. 2).

The organization of the Levites (23:3-32).—Clearly the Chronicler treated this numbering of the Levites as different from the earlier census (21:6). See Numbers 4 for another census of the Levites. According to the Chronicler the Levites were arranged in twenty-four divisions, although it is difficult to determine all twenty-four leaders. There are only twenty-three names preserved. Notice that the descendants of Aaron were excluded from this list because they were not just Levites but the branch of the Levites set apart for priestly service (23:13). The list given here is either limited to those above thirty years of age (v. 3) or those above twenty years of age (v. 24). Perhaps the two numbers reflect different time periods. As time went on it may have become necessary to take younger men in order to have enough.

The Levites were charged with three functions according to the Chronicler: they cared for the buildings and the grounds (v. 28); they helped prepare the offering (v. 29); and, they were part of the musical portion of the worship (v. 30). In the older portion of the Old Testament, such a distinction between Levites who were priests and Levites who were assistants to the priests is not present. Perhaps in the time of the Chronicler such a distinction had become commonplace. Compare the description of the role of the Levites in Numbers 3.

The organization of the priests (24:1-19).—A brief note about the history of the descendants of Aaron introduces this group. For the death of Nadab and Abihu see Numbers 3:4. The main stress lies on the fact that David, with the assistance of two major priestly figures—Zadok and Ahimelech (Abiathar?), organized the priests into twenty-four divisions also. The Zadokites composed twice as many divisions as the descendants of Ahimelech. Apparently the predominence of the Zadokites in the post-exilic community was explained by the book of Samuel as part of God's judgment. See the prophecy of the man of God to Eli (1 Sam. 2:35). Ahimelech was the father of Abiathar. He was slain by Saul. Abiathar became David's lifelong companion until he supported Adonijah against Solomon for the kingship (1 Kings 1:7). The purge of Ahimelech's family by Saul may also explain the difference in numbers between the two families (1 Sam. 22:11-19). Since there was a difference in number between the groups a random selection by lot was used to establish the divisions. The Chronicler listed the leaders of each of the twenty-four divisions (vv. 7-19).

A supplementary list of Levites (24:20-31).—This listing of Levites contains some of the same names just listed. It seems to be a slightly different list that has been retained. Its purpose is not at all clear.

The organization of the musicians (25:1-31).—The same structure existed for the musicians. David organized them also into twenty-four divisions. Asaph, Heman, and Jeduthun (elsewhere called Ethan) represent the three divisions of the Levites

(6:33,39,44). The Chronicler represented their work as that of "prophesying" (v. 1). In the earlier history, music was associated with prophesy. Samuel told Saul he would meet a band of prophets coming down from a worship place with these instruments (1 Sam. 10:5). Thus the role of the prophet in the ancient worship had been completely taken over by the musicians by the time of the Chronicler. Other passages indicate that prophecy had become rare in the later period also (Zech. 13:2).

The organization of the gatekeepers (26:1-19).—The gatekeepers also had twenty-four divisions, although there are twenty-five heads of families listed. The twenty-four groups of gatekeepers were distributed by location rather than by time. Their jobs related them to the gates of the Temple area and to its storehouse. Some of the gatekeepers guarded something called a *parbar* (v. 18), which cannot be located. The word does not seem to be a Hebrew word. It was probably borrowed from the Babylonians and brought back with the returned exiles, but its meaning is still unknown.

Miscellaneous groups (26:20 to 27:34).—The lists which form this long section cover a variety of groups. First there is a list of those who were responsible for the Temple treasuries (26:20-29). The treasury held all the gifts brought home from battle (v. 27) plus all that which the people gave (v. 26). A later section describes the "heads of father's houses" as bringing gifts to Jehiel who had charge of the treasury (29:6-8).

The next group is difficult to interpret. Three men are listed specifically: Chananiah, Hashabiah and Jerijah. They are said to have been appointed to "outside duties" (26:29). They are further related to Israel, the land west of the Jordan and the land east of the Jordan. Perhaps they had something to do with taxation outside the cities; they may have been in charge of customs on roads. The word *outside* sometimes means "street" in Hebrew.

The groups that follow are nonreligious in nature. David's army officers make up the first of these (27:1-15). These names are familiar from the earlier list (chap. 11). Here, however, the army is divided up into twelve divisions, one for each month. According to 1 Kings 4:7 Solomon had twelve officers in charge of gathering food for the king's household. The Chronicler seems to suggest that David also had such an arrangement. If so, nothing else is known of it. In this case the number twenty-four is involved as the size of each division: each division had twenty-four thousand soldiers.

Twelve tribal princes appear in the next group, and these princes are related to the census that David took (27:16-24). This section suggests that David took the census in accordance with the law of the Old Testament, but that the pestilence came anyway. In Numbers 1 the Lord commanded Moses to take such a census of males twenty years old and over. He was to be accompanied by a representative from each tribe, perhaps to insure that younger males were not counted. The Chronicler notes that David had such a group with him and that he did not number those below twenty years of age. Nevertheless, the pestilence struck. The story of the census is in chapter 21.

The list of those who had responsibilities for David's property is a fascinating one, not because of the names of the people, but because of the glimpse it gives us of the life of such a king. Samuel reminded the people of his day what a king could expect to take from the economy of the land (1 Sam. 8:11-18). The passage here indicates the truth of that prophecy. David controlled fields (v. 26), vineyards (v. 27), olive orchards and sycamore trees (v. 28; see also Amos 7:14). He also had herds of sheep (v. 29), camels and she-asses (v. 30). The king's business must have been big business even in that time. All of these people who tilled the land, tended the flocks, and processed the raw materials were dependent on the king for their livelihood. They in turn provided the king with the means to sustain a large group of nobles and army officers who did not provide income to the king directly. At the end of Solomon's reign the people of the northern kingdom did not wish to continue supporting such an elaborate system and rebelled. Some of the people who were supported from David's vast enterprises were those mentioned in verses 32 through 34. Scribes such as Jonathan and Jehiel taught the king's children. Ahithophel and Hushai served as advisers to the king. Joab ran the army.

The Inaugural Ceremony (28:1 to 29:25)

After having described in detail the composition of the groups that made up the inaugural assembly, the Chronicler summarized once again the people involved (28:1). The ceremony as described here would have been an elaborate formal inauguration attended by hundreds of officials who would become responsible to Solomon as the new king.

David's charge to Solomon (28:2-21).—David's address to Solomon falls naturally into four units. It involves first a summary of how Solomon came to the kingship and had the opportunity to build the Temple (vv. 2-8). Next there is a direct charge to Solomon to keep the law and build the Temple (vv. 9-10). The third section (vv. 11-19) involves a description of the plans for the Temple which David provided Solomon. The conclusion of the address consists of David's encouragement to Solomon to start the task of building (vv. 20-21).

David's description of the course of history that led to Solomon's inauguration is virtually a repetition of two earlier statements (17:11-14; 22:7-10). The central message of this speech lies in the emphasis on the legitimacy of Solomon. The Lord himself had narrowed his choice of leaders first to the Southern Kingdom and then to the family of Jesse. Of that family he called David and of "all my sons . . . he has chosen Solomon" (v. 5). Moreover, Solomon was divinely ordained to build the Temple (v. 6). The account of these matters in 2 Samuel gives a detailed picture of the working out of the divine will in and through the palace intrigues surrounding David (2 Sam. 9—20). The Chronicler has chosen to ignore all of that. He has simplified the process by omitting such details. A second noticeable change made here involves the insistence that the continuation of Solomon's kingdom depended on his obedience (v. 7). A comparison with 2 Samuel 7:15-16 shows that this is different. The earlier history described the Lord's promise as unconditional: "your kingdom shall be made sure for ever before me" (2 Sam. 7:16). The Chronicler made that continued success dependent on keeping the commandments; he continued to stress this need for obedience later as the Temple was dedicated (2 Chron. 7:19-22).

As a result of this requirement that the king keep God's law, David urged Solomon to serve the Lord wholeheartedly (28:9-10). These verses echo the language of Deuteronomy 4:25-31 and 6:4.

According to the Chronicler's understanding David had done all of the necessary preparation for building the Temple. He had even received the plans for the Temple "from the hand of the Lord" (v. 19). The plans for each part of the Temple were handed over to

Solomon (vv. 11-13), even down to the amounts of gold and silver
needed for each of the vessels: lampstands, lamps, tables, forks,
basins, cups, and bowls (vv. 14-17). The plans included a design for
a "golden chariot of the cherubim" for the Holy of Holies (v. 18).
Apparently the Chronicler thought of the cherubim as pulling a
chariot and yet somehow covering the ark with their wings. Other
descriptions of the ark and the cherubim may be found in Exodus
25:10-22; 37:1-9; and 1 Kings 6:23-28. Perhaps the vision of Ezekiel
(1:4-28) had influenced the Chronicler, too. Psalm 18:10 also describes the Lord as riding on a cherub and flying.

The chapter ends with words of encouragement for the new king.
David promised him the unfailing help of God (v. 20) and the support of the assembled peoples (v. 21). Solomon needed only to "be
strong and of good courage and do it" (v. 20).

David's charge to the assembly (29:1-9).—David challenged the
assembly to offer its labors and its wealth to the new king for the
great work to be done in building the "palace" (v. 1). The word
palace is not the normal word for the house of the Lord. It is a word
that only appears in the later books of the Old Testament and probably reflects the usage of the Chronicler's own time. David stressed
his own personal contribution, beyond that of the stockpiling of
materials. A talent equalled a weight of about seventy-five pounds.
David's gift, if reckoned at a gold price of about $500 per ounce,
would have been worth close to two billion dollars in the gold alone.
The Chronicler seems to have magnified the size of David's contribution. His point was, however, that David did everything necessary to
get the Temple constructed. The major credit for the construction
belonged to David, even though Solomon actually built the Temple.
The growing reverence for David from whom the Messiah would
come is apparent in the Chronicler's treatment.

The assembled group responded with equal generosity (vv. 6-9).
The *daric* (v. 7) was a Persian coin weighing about one-third of an
ounce. Once again the Chronicler has used a term which was current in his own time but which was not current in David's time.
Jehiel was in charge of the gifts dedicated to God in the later Temple
(26:22).

David's prayer for Solomon (29:10-19).—The essence of David's
prayer is that all the things that the people have been able to give

belonged to the Lord. He expressed thanks that they had been allowed to give them back (vv. 13,16). The Lord is eternal (v. 10), while David and his generation were but passing shadows (v. 15). Therefore, there could be no question of true ownership of wealth on the part of the people. They used God's wealth for a brief period. David prayed that the attitudes of the givers were correct (v. 17) and that the Lord would keep their "purposes and thoughts" properly directed toward him in the future (v. 18). He especially prayed for the king himself that he would keep God's law (v. 19; Deut. 17:18-20).

The crowning of Solomon (29:20-25).—The crowning of Solomon was a worship service in which the people bowed themselves both to God and to the king (v. 20). The following day staggering numbers of animals were sacrificed and offered. Although they offered "burnt offerings" which were wholly consumed in the fire on the altar, they also "sacrificed" animals which they then ate in a joyous celebration (v. 22). The statement that they made Solomon king "the second time" (v. 22) is puzzling, for this is obviously the first time Solomon became king. The statement may be due to a misunderstanding of 1 Chronicles 23:1 which says that David made Solomon king. That verse, however, was a title which introduced the entire account of the crowning. Perhaps a later scribe took that verse to be a reference to an initial crowning and then added the word "second" to verse 22. If this was not the case this reference must remain a puzzle.

Once again the Chronicler has omitted materials about an attempt on Adonijah's part to seize control of the throne from Solomon (1 Kings 1). The reference to Zadok alone without Abiathar is significant. In the attempted revolution Abiathar, David's faithful priest, supported Adonijah instead of Solomon (1 Kings 1:7). As a result of this action Abiathar was banished to his hometown of Anathoth (1 Kings 2:26-27). Thus Zadok took his place beside Solomon (29:22). The officials and the soldiers swore allegiance to Solomon (v. 24) and God blessed Solomon with royal majesty and fame (v. 25).

Summary of David's Reign (29:26-30)

The book of 1 Chronicles comes to an end with this section. See also 2 Samuel 5:5 and 1 Kings 2:11 for statements about the length of David's reign. The Chronicler referred to written works by the three great prophetic figures associated with David: Samuel, Nathan, and Gad. These works do not now exist apart from our books of Samuel, Kings, and Chronicles, which may have been built from these books.